Global Conflict

To Chadwick F. Alger, Michael Banks,
Anthony de Reuck, A.J.R. Groom,
Christopher Hill, Margot Light, Richard
Little, C.R. Mitchell, Robert C. North,
A.N. Oppenheim, Helen Purkitt, Dennis
J.D. Sandole and Matthew R. Willard
who contributed to *Conflict in
World Society,* in response to their
observations and in deep appreciation.

Global Conflict

The Domestic Sources of International Crisis

John W. Burton

Co-Director, Centre for the Analysis of Conflict
University of Kent

Co-Director, The Council for the Facilitation of
International Conflict Resolution
University of Maryland

Wheatsheaf
Books

Center for International Development,
University of Maryland.

First published in Great Britain in 1984 by
WHEATSHEAF BOOKS LTD.
A MEMBER OF THE HARVESTER PRESS GROUP
Publisher: John Spiers
Director of Publications: Edward Elgar
16 Ship Street, Brighton, Sussex

and distributed in the USA by
The Center for International Development,
University of Maryland
College Park 20742

British Library Cataloguing in Publication Data

Burton, John W.
    The general theory of international relations.
    1. International relations
    I. Title
    327   JX1395

ISBN 0-7108-0737-6

Typeset in Parlament Roman by M-Set, 130 Albion St.,
Southwick, Brighton, Sussex
Printed in Great Britain by
Whitstable Litho Ltd., Whitstable, Kent

THE HARVESTER PRESS PUBLISHING GROUP
The Harvester Press Publishing Group comprises Harvester
Press Limited (chiefly publishing literature, fiction, philosophy,
psychology, and science and trade books), Harvester Press
Microform Publications Limited (publishing in microform
unpublished archives, scarce printed sources, and indexes to
these collections) and Wheatsheaf Books Limited (a wholly
independent company chiefly publishing in economics, international politics, sociology and related social sciences), whose
books are distributed by The Harvester Press Limited and its
agencies throughout the world.

Contents

Foreword

By writing *Global Conflict: The domestic sources of international conflict*, John Burton has provided us with a radical intellectual base by which we can judge the quality of the whole social system including the international sub-system. After years of diplomacy and scholarship at its best, he has transmitted to us in a succinct manner the ideas he has learned, invented, practised, written about and taught. The analytical framework provided in this book, and the implications it carries for the study of international relations and foreign policy, are perhaps not any less significant than Keynes' *General Theory of Economics*. I believe that the world is so sociopolitically deformed and crisis-ridden that it requires the creative solutions developed in this book, Burton's 'General Theory'.

Burton writes about the outmodedness of the power politics mode and formulates an analytical framework which focuses on the role of transactions and valued relations in contemporary society. He writes convincingly that the power relations theory cannot explain, for example, why the US fear the sociopolitical developments in Central America any more than they can explain Soviet fear of the events in Poland. He argues that states that employ power to pursue national interests find themselves constrained by valued interactions. Thus, he concludes that power plays only a supportive role in the pursuit of valued relations.

Burton's General Theory in this book argues that the power theorists have it all wrong—the world is hungering to satisfy the identity needs of individuals and groups. Security is not a limited strategic resource, rather, it is abundant and unlimited—the more one is secure, the more everyone else is. Individuals, and ethnic and cultural groups, seek acceptance and recognition in their immediate and larger environments, principally to satisfy their internal needs. The world's international problems are a spillover of the domestic ones and the obverse is true also.

Burton gives interactions and transactions a well-placed prominence in his well-placed General Theory. He posits that cultural and ethnic acceptance in the world, and therefore peace between and within nations, will necessarily increase as a function of the increase in the volume and quality of valued transactions. Thus, politics and policy must engage in designing present and future roles for the members of the international system and interactions which satisfy dearly-held values.

Conflict resolution, following Burton's reasoning, is a complex but rewarding enterprise. It is a process by which conflicting parties are made to see themselves in a win-win situation. Peacemaking events shift from the formalistic and legalistic focus on the single, dramatic events of ceasefires to those of societally and inter-societally valued relationships. It involves, in addition to violence containment acts, learning new norms, establishing positive interactions and designing long-term socioeconomic institutions which reduce structural and behavioural violence in the world.

Whether you agree or disagree with the ideas in this book, you will not be able but to admire Burton for the brilliance with which he writes about the contemporary world, and the role and responsibilities of the superpowers in it.

Edward E. Azar
Center for International Development,
University of Maryland

Preface

This book covers a wide range of topics, which is inevitable when the complex issues of global conflict are being discussed. The focus is finally on domestic political problems and how they spill over into the world system. It is apparent that this is the case in conflicts such as Lebanon and El Salvador. It is less perceived in Soviet-USA relations and in the many conflict situations that are emerging in world society. We tend to define these relationships in terms of great power and ideological rivalries. Yet, finally, it seems that we are led back to domestic system failings and the defence of existing institutions whenever there is a situation of international tension or conflict. This applies to the foreign relations of the Soviet Union and the USA not less than those of the smaller states.

The analysis is made, as explained in the introduction, within a framework that is a departure from traditional and consensus thinking. It will not immediately be acceptable to many practitioners and scholars who operate within a cultural environment that attaches importance to the preservation of political and social structures and institutions as the goal of government. The theoretical foundation of this book is an assertion that there are certain human needs concerned with development, as well as survival, which are ontological and universal. It is these needs which finally determine structures and institutions. Their frustration is a sufficient explanation of political and social instabilities. Policies of intervention and attempts at resolving conflicts fail unless this is taken into account.

Taking the individual as the unit of explanation is a major challenge to traditional Western political thought. The ring of determinism, be it a determinism that stems from human needs, is not always acceptable, especially to so-called 'left' or 'liberal' thinkers. It also has a ring of idealism at first hearing. Whether determinism or idealism or both, this is where contemporary thought and empirical experience are taking us. It is this which is political realism. Western political thinking has been dominated since early Greek and Roman days by the idea that politics was a subjective phenomenon. In more recent language, it is concerned with the authoritative allocation of values. Authorities, élites and rulers had a right to determine values, while others had an obligation to accept their judgments. There was no scientific basis for criticism nor even for comparative assessments between different types of systems and policies. If there are certain ontological human needs, and this now seems to be agreed in the inter-disciplinary literature by implication as we will see, then there is a measure, a reference point for policy and political systems. If such needs exist, then it is idealistic to assume that we can maintain Western types of adversary systems, elitist systems and deterrent strategies to preserve them. They must all be re-assessed and re-conceptualised within this emerging human-needs framework if the conflicts which they create are to be understood and resolved.

Alongside this shift in thinking on the substance of political life, there has been a related shift in thinking about thinking itself. In this study there is little empirical data. The view is adopted that examples that substantiate are of little value. The same examples can be used, by taking different aspects, to refute. The approach in this study is abductive, that is, it is concerned with challenging fundamental assumptions and making re-conceptualisations and deductions from them.

For these two reasons the contemporary scholarly literature has not been found useful, except as a chopping block from time to time. Previous books have dealt with this literature. The study is concerned with an emerging empirical and philosophical paradigm shift. Its validity is in its predictive capacity, its relevance to experience in contemporary world society and its internal logic.

There is one aspect that will concern practitioners and scholars in the Western world, and USA practitioners and scholars in particular. The study is concerned with global conflicts. Soviet-USA relations are clearly important to it. A Western scholar is relatively ill-informed about Soviet affairs, despite Soviet literature and the many opportunities to visit there and to exchange views with visitors from the Soviet Union to many professional associations. There is a tendency, therefore, when discussing systems failings within states to concentrate on Western countries, the USA in particular, whose political systems are better known. However, this is not the reason for what will appear to be a bias underlying 'balanced' statements. There are criticisms of USA structures and policies.

Indeed, this is perhaps the main message of the analytical parts of this study. Recent interventions by the USA in foreign conflict situations have brought little success in terms of the goals sought. They appear to have been both costly and counter-productive. There seem to be three reasons for this. First, the USA has sought to pursue its own security interests, placing them before the values and goals of the nations concerned—and failing to appreciate the limits to power when confronted by such values and goals. National interests have been prejudiced as a result of this. Second, there has been a misunderstanding of the nature of the conflicts in which the USA has been involved and, therefore, of the types of settlement which it has sought to achieve. Third, arising out of this false definition of the situation in which it has been involved, the USA has relied upon force and adversary negotiations where other processes were both appropriate and possible. These three sources of failure all relate back to system failures within USA structures and institutions. They were not due simply to personal mistakes, but reflect some sense that there are philosophical interest positions that must be maintained, come what may.

This study is concerned very much with the dysfunctional

consequences of power-politics, with false definitions of situations and why they occur, and with the processes of conflict resolution that are attuned to the values and needs of parties to disputes. It is the USA that is backing scoundrels all around the globe and their non-legitimized regimes. This leaves the Soviet Union in the happy position of defending and supporting reactions to feudalism and power élites that have little internal support. On a lesser scale they do the same thing for the same reasons. Both have their origins in Western political philosophy which places structures before people. Neither can afford to contemplate a third alternative that would include some of the more benign features of both and promote more effectively the pursuit of human needs. This would be a self-criticism that is not possible in a power-political system. Both, therefore, are defensive under the common pressures of technology and human needs that are drawing them towards a third position—given the avoidance of war. One deduction is that the first of these two great powers that learns and accepts that the individual is finally the unit of explanation will 'win' the competitive rivalry by adapting suitably. An alternative is for both to move in the same direction, and to cease competing with each other. This, then, is a criticism of USA structures and policies, at least as much, if not more, than it is a criticism of Soviet structures and policies. It is fitting in such an introduction to stress that it is not a criticism of Americans and Soviet scholars and administrators. Our problems are not with people and their needs: it is with our thought systems and the circumstances that history has created. Somewhere a development took place that has led civilisations to where they are today: adversary, defensive, elitist, obstructing the evolution that genetically will—given time—lead to changed relationships. The question that is finally posed is whether we have the thought capacity to twist our planned or consciously created structures and institutions to conform more with the forces that will finally destroy them in any event. Given clarity on these issues, then it is more likely that everyone concerned will be prepared to do some costing of the preservation of structures and institutions in the short term. This is what this book is about.

Acknowledgements

This book was commenced while I was 1983 ISA (International Studies Association) Visiting Scholar at the present headquarters of ISA, The Byrnes International Center, University of South Carolina; it was completed while I was a Research Associate at the Center for International Development, University of Maryland.

I wish to express my warm appreciation for the support given me by the Executive Secretary of ISA, Professor James Kuhlman and the 1982-3 President, Professor Harold Jacobson in the promotion of some of the ideas and processes outlined in this book. This support was subsequently extended by Professor Edward Azar, Director of the Center for International Development at Maryland where jointly we were able to apply these processes.

To Professor Chadwick Alger of the Mershon Center, Ohio, I owe special thanks for his permission to quote at length from a talk he gave in 1982 to citizens of Yokohama, Japan. This was published in full in *Cities in Globilization of Human Communities,* YOKE Symposium Report, September 1982. I also wish to thank the editors of the *New York Times* for permission to quote extensively from various reports and articles.

PART I

INTRODUCTION

This book is in four parts with a conclusion. Part I contains an overview and the general approach that is being followed. Part II deals with faults within domestic systems that spill over into the international society. Part III is concerned with the international consequences and reasons why international institutions have failed in their purposes. Part IV is concerned with prescription. The conclusion endeavours to draw the threads together.

We are dealing with complex interactions and events. Unless there is some underlying framework or philosophy, these different variables remain discreet and separate. While Chapter 1 deals generally with the approach and tries to place it in the perspective of the history of thought in the study of international relations; Chapter 2 is designed to provide this with a theoretical-philosophical framework. It is drawn from trends in thought that are now beginning to articulate a philosophy of public policy and to offer some objective guidelines.

1. The Approach

The purpose of this book is to deduce policies and processes that are appropriate in the handling of American-Soviet and global political relations in the longer term. It is an attempt to stand back from the day-to-day events to which the press and politicians react, and to be more analytical and positive. Because policy rests on the definition made of a particular situation, it is necessary, first, to define meaningfully the nature of international relations, that is, to discover why they are as tense and dangerous as they seem to be to both sides.

It is in this latter respect that this book breaks new ground. It is not narrowly about strategy and deterrence to the threats each side poses to the other; it is not about the thermonuclear threat that each side experiences; it is not even about the rivalry between the two different political systems. Rather it is argued that the major sources of potential conflict are the shortcomings within each system that render each insecure, even without any external threat. There are impelling reasons why these internal anxieties spill over into the relations between the two.

This being a new approach to relations between states, and American-Soviet relations in particular, it is appropriate to explain shortly the stages of development that have taken place in the study of international relations. After the failure of the League of Nations and the outbreak of the second world war, international lawyers, and scholars generally, were disillusioned. They reacted sharply against a law-and-order approach for the control of the international system. They moved towards a power-politics explanation of relations between states. They gave up any hope that an international system could be built in the image of a national community and settled for a system of anarchy in which relations would be determined by the relative power of states. [1] As one scholar termed it, their thinking was in accord with a 'billiard ball model',[2] each separate state reacted to others, the larger determining the behaviour of the smaller. Contact was on the external surface, and international relations could be studied as a subject quite separately from domestic politics. Indeed, this approach was reflected in the United Nations' Charter drafted in 1945, which included a clause that provided that what went on inside any member state was a matter of domestic jurisdiction and not the concern of the organisation.[3]

By the 1960s it had become apparent that this was an over-simplification. Without denying the importance of relative power, a school of thought developed that attached importance to communications and transactions across state boundaries, many of which were outside state control. Such transactions had increased enormously as a result of wartime technological advances. The concept of the 'billiard ball model' gave place to the 'cobweb model'.[4] This drew attention to the network of systems and transactions that cut across state boundaries and make the international state system into a world society. Theories—or observations of reality—emerged that emphasised nations' interdependence and these came to be more prominent than power theories.

This was an important advance in thought for it recorded the reality that states were not concerned only with the acquisition of power, either for defence or for expansion, but were also concerned with transactions that were valued. This meant that there were constraints on the exercise of power, constraints that are inherent in the values that they attach to these transactions. A theory emerged that suggested that states do all that is within their power to pursue their national interests, but are limited in the use of that power by the need to promote and to maintain, as part of these interests, valued interactions in trade, technology, partnerships in defence and other areas. By implication, power was no longer seen to be an end in itself, or even as a means to primary goals of expansion or aggression. Power was a fall-back position in the pursuit of national interests, the more important components of which were valued relationships.

This approach had its counterpart in 'control theory' which sociologists were putting forwards in the 1970s to explain deviant behaviour within the framework of behaviour generally. The theory was that there are certain human needs to be pursued, ontological needs associated with development, and that individuals or groups use all means at their disposal, legal or illegal, to pursue these, constrained only by the values they attach to relationships with others in society.[5] The shocks of Vietnam and Iran, the inability of the USA to control the behaviour of Israel in Lebanon, and of repressive élites in Central America and elsewhere, gave credence to this view. Power was limited; the great powers were powerless giants in circumstances in which smaller states had their own values to pursue and in which the great powers valued their relationships with them.

By the 1980s, however, it became clear that, whatever importance was attached to power and to transactions, and however these two phenomena were able to explain some aspects of inter-state behaviour, they were inadequate. A power-relationships theory could not explain the real fear the USA had of reforms being sought in Central America by those opposing repressive and feudal regimes. The absence of direct or even indirect Soviet influence on any significant scale eliminated a strategic motivation on the part of the US to support existing repressive regimes. There had to be another reason. So, too, in the case of Poland: there had to be a reason outside strategy that made the Soviet fear the consequences of developments there.

Events in world society generally, and the behaviour of smaller states, required explanations that could not adequately be deduced from considerations of power and constraints on the exercise of power. World society was characterised by ethnic conflicts within and between states, by race riots, by high levels of street violence in the great and small powers, by high levels of unemployment and growing inequalities of income and opportunity. Non-aligned governments, in addition to others, sought foreign assistance in maintaining themselves in power. Many states relied on their military forces to prevent political change. The military equipment they sought from the great powers was for internal control as often as it was for national defence. There were clearly forces at work within the world society that could not be explained by reference to national power and the constraints imposed by transactions with other nations. Something was missing.

The missing element was the relationship between domestic and international politics. The original, classical assumption that international relations could be studied as a separate discipline, that domestic politics was a matter of domestic jurisdiction, was a false one. It was always agreed that there was a connection between domestic and international. Periods of history were written around particular national leaders and their foreign exploits. It was always clear that greater powers found it necessary to intervene in the affairs of smaller states in their own strategic interests, and this could be coped with within the power-politics model. There was always a study of 'comparative politics' which gave international relations scholars the opportunity to compare and consider the international consequences of different forms of government and different policies and styles. What was missing was a realisation that those in power within states feel that they must go to great lengths, even to war, in defending their systems and institutions against change, external influences, and the modifications that international transactions and exchanges of knowledge can promote. In the West continuing unemployment, gross inequalities in income and opportunity, high levels of violence in social life and a host of related problems were being experienced. Political parties were moving toward extreme positions—for change or in defence of the *status quo*. Demands for change at home could not be resisted if neighbouring countries and allies within spheres of influence undertook reforms to resolve similar internal problems. Thus, the US gave support to corrupt and repressive regimes within its own sphere of influence and elsewhere, even though there was little evidence of direct, or even indirect, Soviet intervention. The fear that the world would 'go communist' was a fear that the western-type free enterprise system was not meeting the needs of the peoples concerned. It was convenient to blame communist and Soviet influence from Southern Africa to Central America.

Similarly, the Soviet Union continually claimed American intervention in its sphere of influence. While in both cases there is little doubt—though little hard information—that there were some interventions, direct or indirect, they were not the explanation of unrest and subversion within the spheres of influence of the two great powers. Changes within spheres of influence and elsewhere in world society were seen to be a threat to one system or the other because of the need for change within each.

Consequently we need to add a new dimension. In addition to power and to values attached to transactions, there is a need to give attention to the system failures and inadequacies of both capitalism and socialism. Indeed, it is arguable that this is the major factor, a sufficient explanation, of great power rivalry in the 1980s.

More traditional international historians may react to this approach by quoting cases of sheer aggression, such as that of Hitler's Germany and Tojo's Japan. A situation, having been perceived within a particular theoretical framework, is difficult to re-perceive. The power explanations of the second world war are adequate only within the memory of the times, aggressive behaviour that had to be contained. However, a reassessment within an alternative framework focuses attention on other origins of war. The Japanese case is a clear one. Britain, endeavouring to export its severe unemployment in the cotton industries, closed its markets to Japan. This, and many other parallel moves by Britain and other colonial powers, left a Japan that had conformed with international trading norms without sources of raw materials and markets. It sought a co-prosperity sphere. It probably had no option in terms of economic survival, despite the risks. The struggles of Germany after the first world war showed how massive unemployment could lead to aggressive foreign policies. Without arguing these cases, the suggestion is made only that a new emphasis on the domestic origins of international conflict could alter our perceptions of past events, and that these perceptions should not lead us to dismiss richer explanations of current problems.

Psychologists and others who deal with conflictual relations among persons and small groups will recognise immediately the approach being adopted. External conflict is so often a projection of inner problems. Whether it be individuals, small groups or nations, such an approach has far-reaching implications for policy. If conflicts were for reasons of scarcity of materials, shortage of space or an absence of relationships, then some coercive system backing up agreed norms of behaviour would be a remedy. If, on the other hand, conflict were because of some failings within the units interacting, some insecurities inherent within them, then the required remedies would be different. No amount of threat or coercion would contain the conflictual behaviour.

These shifts in thought have not been discontinuities. The shift from an emphasis on power to one on communications was made in the light of technological developments and experience, yet still remained within the framework of power. The cybernetics aspect of decision-making that were emphasised in the early 1960s[6] was an extension of power theory. Economies in the use of power were possible by reason of feedback mechanisms. The shift in thought from communications to the constraints imposed by relationships was also a recognition of developments in the world society, in particular far greater levels of transactions and greater dependencies. So, too, the shift to a focus on domestic systems and their failings reflects a further stage in the development of societies, greater demands for participation, increased assertion of human rights and needs, the lessened abilities of central authorities to control behaviour of greater and more complex population groups with means of violence readily at hand. Such a focus does not detract from the importance of relative power, transactions and dependency as explanations of national behaviour in the world system. It is an addition that synthesises these different aspects.

All manner of issues are raised at the international level when this approach is adopted. For instance, we could deduce that there cannot be successful arms negotiations until there is a lessened felt need for arms and, furthermore, that this will not occur until internal changes are made that render each system more secure. It is implied that both capitalism and socialism, as they have developed, are defective in some ways, causing domestic concerns which conveniently are blamed on the other. It raises the question whether each system requires the cooperation of the other in solving domestic problems. It points to the need for time in which adjustments can be made, and it suggests the dangers in trying to exacerbate the difficulties of the opposing side. The question is raised whether the political processes of the systems, and the élites associated with these processes, are a source of system failure and, therefore, of international tension. The approach raises the question whether governments and élites, which may be a source of problems in relationships, are in a position to handle relationships, or whether they require inputs from others and processes of analysis and consultation outside the traditional policy-forming and diplomatic bargaining procedures.

Are the two systems that are in competition so rigid that they are unlikely to alter in response to technological change and to human values, towards some common third position? If so, what causes such rigidity—élite defence, an absence of perceived options, fear of extremes? Are the two systems so mutually incompatible that there can be no peaceful cooperation pending change and adaption to circumstances?

There seem to be three possibilities. One, the two systems are so mutually incompatible, and in such immediate competition, that they pose a direct threat to each other. Second, the two systems are not objectively a threat to each other, but for a variety of historical and cultural reasons are perceived to be so. The third possibility combines the first two. The two systems both have domestic failings that are becoming more serious with time. Rather than acknowledge the challenge to their capitalist and socialist ideologies and institutions, and the challenge to leadership that is implied, each blames the other for their internal deficiences. Both sense that even the existence of the other poses a threat, particularly when there is close geographical proximity and peoples can learn at first hand the good points of the alternative system.

It is this last explanation that seems to accord most with both reason and experience. There is system schizophrenia that gives rise to leadership paranoia: there is a condition of apprehension and suppressed self-criticism that leads to loss of confidence and to fear.

It is difficult for someone with limited knowledge of what goes on in the life of the Soviet peoples to make judgements on the adequacy of the Soviet system. It does seem to be true that there is a high level of frustration and boredom in its society, which appear to give rise to problems of alcoholism, lack of enthusiasm in production, envy of outsiders and a degree of political dissent despite severe controls. The problems in the West are no less severe. There is persistent unemployment with all manner of side-effects, and frustration and boredom among young people who cannot find jobs or a place in society. There is violence in the streets at an unacceptable level. There are gross inequalities of income, in opportunity and even in life-expectation. There are city riots, race riots, and organised crime and corruption, even at high political levels. Despite affluence in some sectors of society, there are inadequate resources available for public health and education.

These symptoms of something being wrong in the free enterprise system as it has developed are met with appeals for law and order and by increased coercion. Jails are full, but the level of crime does not diminish. With more and more repression, more infringement of those liberties the system is supposed to feature, including freedom of information, with more defensive reactions, a sense of failure is promoted. For political reasons the explanation of failure cannot be attributed to the system itself. It has to be attributed, in red herring style, to an alien or outside influence.

We are, in the West, fully aware of such system defects, and apparently élites, perhaps because they are isolated from them, are prepared to live with them. Press headlines read 'Mental Anguish of the Young Unemployed'. Articles are written about the suicide and mental illness rates among the young unemployed. The plight of the permanently unemployed and the aged are common topics for discussion. We brace ourselves against an upsurge of violence and personal problems as the frustrations grow. Child abuse and family problems generally associated with stress are constantly before us. We are aware of the revolt of 'rich kids', though we cannot understand why privileged people should behave this way. All of these symptoms of something being wrong appear to increase with time. It has to be deduced that at some point organised society will be disrupted.

Awareness, however, has not led to relevant corrective policies, despite the longer-term projections that can be made. It would be necessary to effect radical changes in social policies and economic structures if these problems were to be tackled. For this reason, the analysis of crime and of dissidence within contemporary societies are not subjects that can be dealt with seriously. The acceptable remedies are those that fall within the consensus of a law-and-order framework. Existing structures and institutions must be maintained, in particular the economic structures, be they capitalist or socialist. The more the existing structures are bolstered, the greater the problem.

The West is beginning to face a crisis of confidence at a political level. The democratic electoral process is seen to rest to an increasing degree on the funding that is possible for candidates and political parties. Even so, the final outcome is likely to be a government with a mandate from less than 50 per cent of the electorate. Once elected, a government acts as though it has a right to pursue the policies of its choosing, even when there is a clear public opinion in opposition. The majority rule notion is, in any event, difficult to justify in conditions, widespread in modern world society, in which there are significant ethnic and cultural differences.

Such criticisms apply no less to socialism in its contemporary form. Socialism now has a tarnished image. In the 1930s a high proportion of thoughtful people, young and old, were socialist. Socialism was the accepted long-term answer to economic and political problems, and to the problem of war. Christianity and socialism were frequently equated. However, contemporary forms of socialism are no less élite-dominated than are forms of democratic capitalism. Socialism is not the participatory system it was once thought to be.

The reality is that civilisations are still at a primitive stage and running into problems that cannot be solved without radical changes in thought and practice. If not solved they are likely to set in motion responses that are destructive and without positive goals. Political theory is as yet inadequate, and political practice is universally élitist and lacking the legitimacy necessary for stability. It is a crisis stage: highly organised societies have evolved, creating just those conditions that prevent the further evolution that is required for their survival.

A contemporary perspective, stimulated by contemporary events, including violent challenges to authorities, communal conflicts and behaviour that is labelled 'deviance', forces us to challenge many normative, classical assumptions. We can no longer assume that there is something natural and sanctified about 'legal' authority and its coercive institutions. We are being forced by events to accept a notion of legitimacy based, not on legality, but upon the view that legitimacy is measured by the degree to which authorities and institutions serve those over whom the authority is exercised and, in particular, by the degree to which they promote the identity, development and a sense of fulfilment of the people. Failure in this, leading to disaffection, is likely to lead to coercion by authorities, making the position worse. Problems inherent in the system are thereby settled but not resolved. Finally, coercive settlements become physically impossible.

This is not an observation based on idealism or humanitarianism. It is the politically realistic observation that, unless there is development and fulfilment of needs of individuals and groups, unless problems are solved and the need for coercion avoided, a social and political order may not be stable and harmonious, no matter what the levels of coercion. Protest movements, violence at all social levels, terrorism, communal conflicts, dissident behaviour, strikes, revolts, revolutions and wars are observable symptoms of unobservable motivations and needs. Labelling and suppressing behaviour does not disguise the needs for structural changes.

It is in this perspective that we need to examine US-USSR relations, and world society in general. Our problems are not mainly international in the sense that there are some unique features of relations between states that lead to tension and to conflict. Our international problems are a spillover of domestic problems. Universally, we are fearful of survival of our political systems, leaders are fearful of their own role survival, privileged groups are defensive of their positions in their types of society. Competing systems, alien philosophies, no matter what their attributes, are perceived as a threat. Capitalism and communism are a threat to each other, not because the authorities in each threaten each other, but because each feels threatened by its own failings. This is conspicuously so of patently unstable societies such as South Africa, and societies around the world which would not survive without external support. It is as true, though on a different time-scale, of the leading states in the two rival camps.

A 'no fault' approach is the appropriate one to adopt. Both systems have problems to solve; both are subject to technological and human pressures that will force changes in time, most likely in the same direction; both require insights, creative thinking and, most of all, time. Intellectually, there is reason for the utmost cooperation between the leaders and the peoples of the two systems to assist in the process and to provide time. Politically, the drive is to take advantage of whatever weaknesses the one discerns in the other, even though the outcome is likely to be a defensive war. This power-politics approach is outmoded. The elements of transactions, valued relationships that arise out of them, and system adjustments are missing from this 1940s power approach to world politics.

Events that have taken place even during the writing of this book have helped to clarify the problem and to redefine the nature of great power conflict. The breakdown of the arms

negotiations in 1983 was not primarily because of any failure
to arrive at an agreement. It became clear that, had
negotiations succeeded beyond all expectations, there would
have been no significant change in strategic relationships.
Substantial reductions in arms levels would still have left
over-kill capacities. Meanwhile, attention had been focused
on the internal problems of many states and regions,
especially of the Middle East and Central America. Lebanon,
El Salvador, North-South Korea relations and many others
demonstrated that the core problem in Soviet-American
relations is the absence of any global stability due to
feudalism, oppression, undevelopment, absence of identity
where ethnicity is a factor, and such fundamental conditions
that are largely out of the control of the great powers in the
short term. The terrorism that accompanies these situations
was perceived by the US as a new weapon, a Soviet weapon.
Defence budgets had to be large enough to cope with many
wars and confrontations globally at one and the same time—a
tremendous and probably an impossible cost. The January
1984 Kissinger Report on Central America recognised this in
so far as it recommends economic aid as a means of dealing
with political unrest and 'communism'. At the same time
there was a recommendation for increased military support
for regimes under threat—regardless of their repressive
nature. This duality was a symptom of confusion, and
evidence that changes in definition were taking place as the
real nature of the situations became apparent. While the US
found difficulty in acknowledging system failings in its
sphere of influence, and while the Soviet Union was no less
reluctant to accept the need for increased participation in its
sphere, failure to control, failure to maintain regimes,
stimulated rethinking. It was not nuclear threat that was the
source of conflict, but system failings in the two competing
ideologically-based structures.

In Part II we shall be examining some of the system failings
that seem to be at the root of East-West tensions. First,
however, it is necessary to provide the theoretical framework
which leads both to the identification of the system failures
that are significant, and to the means of dealing with
them. This is the subject of the next chapter.

NOTES

1. In the USA the leader in this field was Hans J. Morgenthau, the author of probably the most widely read text in international relations, *Politics among Nations: The struggle for peace and power*. In Britain the power politics school was also led by an international lawyer and refugee from Germany, Georg Schwarzenberger, who wrote *Power Politics: A study of world society*. The titles indicate the simple cynicism which was their theme.

2. See Arnold Wolfers, *Discord and Collaboration*, in which this model was used to depict the power politics approach.

3. The domestic jurisdiction clause 7 of Article 2, was agreed as an amendment at the Charter Conference on the submission of the Australian delegation which feared interference in its 'white Australia policy' (now abandoned).

4. The cobweb model was introduced by John Burton in his *World Society* to emphasise the transactional nature of contemporary world society.

5. For an exposition of control theory, see Paul Sites, *Control, the Basis of Social Order*.

6. See Karl Deutsch in his imaginative book *The Nerves of Government*.

2. The Philosophy of Public Policy

We are concerned with domestic policies and their impact on relations between states. Domestic policies, in turn, reflect political structures and management of political affairs. In order to make a critical assessment of policies and alternatives it is necessary, therefore, to have some basis, some reference points, so that assessments are not merely subjective judgements.

The classical—and the contemporary—position as far as political practice is concerned is that there can be no objective assessment of political policies. Politics is concerned with the authoritative allocation of values. Values are subjective judgements or priorities. Competing approaches may seek to achieve the 'general will' or the 'common good', but there can be no objective assessments of differing values, goals or policies.

This classical approach to the problem of policy assessment has been fully dealt with by many scholars. Brecht[1] describes how at the end of the last century the question asked was 'What are the ends of state and of government?' or, 'What is the best form of government?' The answers were in 'ought' terms: governments *ought* to serve the interests of the greatest number of individuals; states *ought* to be sovereign. In this century, philosophers and political scientists began to be self-conscious about the need not to make such value judgements. They were concerned with facts and logical reasoning. They had no basis on which to pass judgements on repression, forms of government or ideologies. There developed all manner of means by which to overcome this problem, in particular to ignore it or to refer to norms or to democratic principles. Nevertheless, the consensus has been that there is no objective basis of assessment of competing policies or systems.

This is one reason why domestic politics have not been analysed as a source of international conflict. If there is no means of assessing competing or different policies, there is little point in seeking to pin-point responsibility. Hitler's Germany clashed with the rest of Western Europe; but there was no means by which responsibillity for war could be attributed to Germany or to any other state. All were acting in their own perceived interests, within their own value systems.

In this book we are adopting a contrary viewpoint. We are seeking to determine those structures and policies that are a source of international tension and conflict. The implication is that there is some means of assessment of policies, some discoverable source of conflict that spills over into the international system. This implies a theory of behaviour that is as scientific as theories in the physical sciences. It implies that there are certain ontological aspects of behaviour that are predictable, certain features of behaviour that are not influenced by subjective judgements and cannot be controlled. There are certain requirements of the individual that *must* be met if social organisations are to be stable. This reflects a paradigm shift that has been taking place in the political and social sciences in the last few decades. It makes a new approach to international politics possible. Hence the need to state in some detail the theoretical framework and the assumptions underlying the argument.

The classical problem that remains with us emerged because authorities, the type of system and institutions that prevail, have been the focus of attention. Accordingly, political theory has been concerned primarily with organisations and their preservation. In the classical view of society there are those who have a right to expect obedience and those who have a moral duty to obey.[2] In some societies this classical view leads to criticism of regimes being treated as dissident behaviour. It is a necessary assumption inherent in this view that the individual is a malleable unit, subject to a socialisation process managed by the state.

It is not surprising, therefore, that the individual as a participant in society has received little analytical attention from political philosophers. On the contrary, a special type of 'man' has been invented to fit in with the theories and models of social organisation that have been developed.

For example, economists invented 'economic man', a unit, a person or a firm designed to have just those attributes that would be required by the smooth running, self-regulating private enterprise system modelled by economists. Joan Robinson has said it was not the role of economists to make critical assessments about social consequences; it was their right to justify what had evolved. They assumed that man was suited to the free enterprise system and it was suited to 'him'. This unit was rational, made choices such that non-material values were downgraded and created this ideal-type economic system.

The lawyer's individual, also, had the necessary attributes to benefit from and make ideal a system of law and order in which those in authority had a right to rule and to expect others to obey. Legal 'man' was rational, and responded to the cost benefits of conformity and deterrants. Only the demented and the demonic were incapable of appreciating that it was in the common interest and, therefore,the individual interest, to conform to the legal norms that prevailed. In the legal view society's interests and the interests of the individual are identical, even though society is managed by a class of persons which has the right to govern and coerce. (A contemporary political view is that this philosophy is confined to communism and to the Soviet in particular. There may be some special cultural factors operating there; but the general classical approach prevails in the practices of the West also.)

Even the psychologist's individual prompts the question, 'why are only *some* individuals deviant'? It seems to be assumed that there are attributes of deviants that lead them to confront legal norms. The 'normal' individual is conformist by nature, or at least subject to successful socialisation.

The view that the individual is or should be malleable is not confined to those seeking to maintain social systems. There are those who assume the need for change toward egalitarianism, a redistribution of income and alterations in the control of production who, no less, create a human being who has those interests, values and preferences that fit into their political ideologies. Whether the orientation is toward conservation or revolution, in both cases the individual has been assumed to be a malleable unit, one that is or can be adapted to the needs of the system. The goal can be either system preservation or system change; but in neither case is satisfaction of human values or needs of primary importance.

It could be that the individual, defined by reference to some universal human needs that will be pursued over the longer term regardless of constraints, needs such an identity and participation, serves well as the basis of an explanation of social change and of the consequences of resistance to social change. Indeed, the contemporary literature is moving strongly in this direction, thanks to the disruptions to societies that we are observing. There are altering concepts, changing emphases and a-disciplinary approaches that are giving rise to an alternative paradigm. Twentieth century experience has persuaded observers and writers that the individual may be an independant variable, that there may be no institutional devices, rule-governed norms or organisational influences that can contain his ontological propensities. Generalisations, explanations and predictions are possible once universal patterns of behaviour are discovered. Assessments can be made as to whether policies are self-defeating, likely to destroy social organisation, and as to whether certain properties of systems and means of management of systems are sources of conflict.

This emerging theoretical framework has been spelled out elsewhere in recent publications. [5] Traditional thought regarded positive law as being legitimised by its operation: it was through the pursuit of the 'common good' that the individual would benefit most. Positive law had, therefore, to be defended and enforced. However, this philosophy did not take sufficiently into account that social institutions and the definitions of the 'common good' reflected class, and not necessarily common good interests. The current return to the individual as the unit of concern is not because of some vague notion of natural justice; it is a concern that there are needs that must be satisfied if the individual within the social system is to be supportive of it. In the tension between human needs and institutions, it is change in institutions that is required. The organisational — individual debate is being resolved by a synthesis, by a focus on the individual unit to the extent that the needs of the unit determine the effective operation of the social system of which it is a part. The goal is the positive law goal of a harmonious society in which the units adapt to changing environmental conditions, but only within the limits set by the need for the satisfaction of human needs.

It is within this framework that we can isolate those system faults that are rendering contemporary societies, East and West, fragile and fearful. The issue is not one of competing ideologies or systems, it is the extent to which each system is failing to achieve its own goals. There are some features in each that are benign, some that are malign. It is this framework that enables us to determine which are which.

There is another philosophical consideration that is a feature of the approach adopted, and that is the way in which the analysis is made. This relates to the assertion that there can be a theory of behaviour from which it is possible to arrive at conclusions about behaviour even in the absence of empirical evidence. For example, if there are certain human needs that *will* be pursued and if there are circumstances that frustrate the pursuit of such needs, it can be deduced that there will be behavioural responses that are predictable, and responses, when they occur, that can be explained within this theoretical framework.

This is, once again, a departure from usual treatments. Western scholarship — especially American scholarship — is greatly concerned with data and the manipulation of data as a means of explanation and verification. We are here dealing with two political systems that are in sharp conflict because of highly political ideological differences. Each side accuses the other of malign intentions. The relationship long passed the stage at which there was an interest in finding out accurately whether or not the other side was malign or not. It entered into the dangerous stage in which both assume the other to be malign, when the Cold War emerged after the cooperation of the second world war. The present stage is concerned with how to defend against or defeat the other side. Even the competitive side of détente has given way to the stage in which both sides believe that they have to 'win'—not by competition, but by power and strategy — if they are to survive.

These changes have taken place because of experience, because of the 'facts', because of statements and deeds that have been interpreted within an ideological framework. Every move the other side makes can be interpreted as malign. An arms control initiative by one side that may have been intended to be conciliatory, is necessarily interpreted as a trick or some sophisticated bargaining move to achieve a malign intention.

This is the problem of inductive reasoning, of coming to conclusions on the basis of observed evidence. Policy-makers, working within their ideological frameworks, responding to day-to-day situations, are concerned with observable data. They are flooded with intelligence reports and advice that are data-based. They have little but their ideological framework in which they can interpret and analyse these data. An aircraft that strays into foreign territory is immediately perceived by the authorities concerned as a likely enemy spy-plane, while its shooting-down is perceived by the other side as evidence of inhumanity. The total data are never available, and ideological selections are made from whatever data are avail-able.

It will be seen that in the analysis some attention is paid to the consequences of such decision-making for foreign policy relations. However, the deductive approach followed in the exposition has wider implications. Arguments are based on deductive reasoning very largely to the exclusion of example in many cases: for every example there can always be quoted a counter-example or some data that contradict the example given.

The approach adopted is strongly a 'no-fault' one. It is not possible to 'blame' the Soviet or American leadership for the present dangerous state of relations between the two countries. Each side is responding to events in the best way it knows, within the knowledge framework at its disposal, in the pursuit of its own interests. Even war, with all its implications, could not be 'blamed' on either side. If we were to attach blame in the future it will not be to politicians or to élites that support political leaders. It will be to scholars who are fully aware of the inductive-deductive problem of analysis, and who have chosen to give so little attention to it in their endeavours to reach conclusions without a scholarly examination of their own ideological and philosophical assumptions. They have very readily been absorbed into the framework of decision-makers, sometimes taking part in sophisticated data or intelligence gathering exercises that must be, by their nature, dysfunctional and finally destructive of the goals their political leaders seek to achieve. It is not data that are lacking, but means of interpretation, that is, an adequate theoretical framework. Even this is no longer lacking in the literature of the behavioural sciences. It is lacking in the tool-kit that teachers and advisers of governments choose to use.

It was at the end of the last century that a self-employed intellectual, and son of a Harvard mathematics professor,[6] pointed to the way out of this problem. Gathering information that supports a contention is obviously a deception when contrary evidence is readily available. Having a theory and interpreting from it is obviously misleading unless there are opportunities for falsifying the theory by some adequate tests—which in the international field are not available. How does one test whether deterrent threats and strategies deter? How can one know that the thermonuclear deterrent is in fact a deterrent? The way out, in the view of this scholar is 'abduction', or a searching analysis and examination of our original hypotheses, our conceptual notions and assumptions and prejudices.

This modern scholars have failed to do and, as a consequence, practitioners have not had brought to their attention the implications of their rhetoric and their reasoning. What is democracy? Majority government that can suppress the natural aspirations of different ethnic communities? Elections through which sometimes less than 25 per cent of the total electorate vote for the presidential candidate? What is freedom? Freedom of expression only, while there are controls on the freedom of information? What is social justice? The availability equally to all of educational and medical facilities? In political theory, what is the common good, and whose role is it to determine it? Are there those who have a right to rule and others who have a moral obligation to obey? And how are these two categories to be selected? The almost unquestioning acceptances of a great deal of traditional political theory and the assumptions that are part of it that characterise western higher learning is a 'blame' that needs to be placed, even within a no fault approach.

It is understandable that a paradigm shift is resisted. There were many vested interests that made scholars reluctant to accept a round earth. They were correct in refusing to accept the early empirical evidence as presented to them. But even a theoretical explanation was difficult to accept despite its explanatory power. So, too, in contemporary scholarship. A dramatic paradigm shift has taken place in the behavioural sciences, yet scholars in large numbers are reluctant to accept it as it undermines their professional interests in data manipulation and their career interests in advising. Rather they choose the politics of academia, fought out tightly within an inductive framework in which 'data' relating to persons and performance determine 'truth'. Meanwhile, two great powers face each other, each perceiving a malign intent, each believing that survival rests on the destruction of the other. Both can call on scholarship to support their stance, and both are provided with powerful, and powerfully-manipulated, 'data'.

This philosophical issue is different from the political

phenomenon of deliberate misinformation, and deliberate selection of data to justify a position. But the two are related: both have the result of misinformation and sometimes it is difficult to determine whether there is or is not a deliberate intent to mislead and to distort. Take, for example, American claims to uphold freedom and justice. In the name of freedom and democracy the United States gives strong support to authorities in countries where there are repressive regimes, and seeks to destabilise some that are clearly democratic and liberal, such as a former government in Chile and a Labour government in their ally, Australia.[7] These interventions appear to be conscious acts that could be labelled aggressive, and about which one could be cynical. They are all due, at least in part, to the unconscious selection of facts that is a feature of inductive thinking. While they can be justified on strategic or national interest grounds, they can, no less, be argued to be self-defeating of their goals. There is lacking an adequate theoretical framework of decision-making and a dangerous absence of deductive or abductive thinking.

A good deal of attention is given in this study, therefore, to the practical problem of determining motivations and intentions in ways that offset inductive conclusions arrived at within an ideological thought system.

NOTES

1. See the introductory pages of this classic on *Political Theory*. It sets out the problems that philosophers have faced in a stark form.
2. The English lawyer Lord Dennis Lloyd presents the classical view in *The Idea of Law*.
3. See Chapter 6 for quotes and references.
4. See S. Himmelweil, 'The individual as basic unit of analysis'.
5. In particular, see J. Burton, *Deviance, Terrorism and War*, Chapter 3.
6. C.S. Peirce.
7. It is always difficult to quote firm evidence in these cases and the author relies here on personal experiences as a former Foreign Office official. However, some details are given in Robert Lindsey's account of his experiences. See *The Falcon and the Snowman*, p.163.

PART II:

SYSTEM FAULTS

The underlying theme has been revealed in Part I: it is, in short, that ultimately, if societies are to be stable and harmonious, structures must be adapted to the needs of the persons who compromise them, rather than the other way around.

In this Part, we are concerned with a variety of system faults that are common to all contemporary political systems, and which lead to internal unrest and tensions in their relationships with others. They range from personality problems of leaders to the evolution of structures that become dysfunctional. We begin to find an explanation of disruptive behaviour at all levels.

What is striking when we begin to think about our contemporary problems, domestic and international, is that we are led inevitably to challenge many of our traditional ways of looking at social organisation. Notions with which we have felt comfortable—democracy, legality, the rights of central authorities to enforce law and order, the common good—no longer provide us with a basis for consensus. We are faced with a paradigm shift: the world is no longer flat and we have to accommodate to a new notion, roundness. This is the nature of the shift in thinking that is required if we are to resolve the problems of survival with which civilisations are currently faced.

3. Personalities and Politics

Personalities and élites are facts of political life. Consideration of sources of system failures invites the question whether contemporary systems are dealing adequately with the consequences of personality and élite influences that may not be benign. To what extent are authoritarian personalities and their simplistic solutions a source of domestic and international problems, and to what extent are élites responsible?

History and contemporary accounts of political events focus on personalities. Interpretations of events and predictions tend to be based on assessments of the behaviour of leaders. Consequently, the personality role problem—that is, the extent to which the one affects the other—has been much discussed.[1] It could be that the selection process in a political system favours a certain type of leadership in particular circumstances. The charismatic independence leader enacts one role, the more policy-oriented another. Whether circumstances create the leader or whether leaders alter conditions, there are clearly situations in which role and occupant are out of phase. The charismatic or wartime leader is likely to outlive the special circumstances that placed him/

her in that role. Some systems make possible the exercise of dictatorial powers by leaders who achieve an authority role by force. Personalities must be treated as a significant influence in political life in all systems of which we have had experience.

In the wide range from analytical and cautious leadership of the Attlee and Kennedy type to the extremes of dictatorial authority, it is possible to locate the authoritarian personality in politics. It is never clear whether situations require and attract authoritarian personalities, or whether such personlities create situations that seem to justify their presence. It would seem to be the former. For example, Stalin is associated with a stage of development that seemed to require major contemporary sacrifices for future development. Hitler is associated with post-war unemployment and national loss of identity. Whichever is the case, the fact is that such personalities emerge from time to time in all political systems: sometimes with disastrous consequences.

The authoritarian personality is characterised by particular attributes. The dominant features are persistence, certainty, rigidity and inflexibility in the pursuit of simple solutions to complex problems. In politics this tends to lead to the use of threat, coercion and force to eliminate opposition and opposing opinions.

The authoritarian personality is a general phenomenon in all walks of life. It is of particular significance in political life for three reasons. First, it is of the nature of politics that there need be no relevant professional qualifications. There are, therefore, none of the constraints that are experienced by persons who work within a discipline or body of specialised knowledge. There are no objective reference points by which to assess the validity of authoritative decisions. They rest on their own base, that is, the power that can be exercised in their implementation. Second, an authoritative personality in a political leadership role has the power of the state at his/her disposal. Third, publics are attracted by simple solutions, simply articulated, at least until failure results in unacceptable costs and consequences. Typically, these costs have to be high in terms of suffering before publics turn and, even then, the turnaround is a slow process and actively resisted by such leadership.

In the early 1980s the authoritarian personality was one of the elements in the dangerous state of relations between the USSR and USA and some of its allies. The US President was a leader featuring a high moral stance, clear right-wrong values, and solutions by force. Never were doubts or complexities presented. Inconsistencies and factually incorrect statements were incorporated into such stances and value statements.[2] In the British case, the leadership marked a discontinuity in tradition. The ·paternalistic, aristocratic leadership of the Tory Party that relied on a confident, somewhat flexible and experienced establishment gave place to a lower-middle-class leadership that shared the American philosophy of the role of the individual in an achieving society. Norms were power or success norms. Right and wrong were clearly defined by these norms.

Probably prevailing conditions, especially economic conditions and a sense of failure in the political and economic systems, were responsible for the selection in both cases. Soviet leadership is less easy to assess. Circumstances there seemed to have led to attempts to find a more professional leadership, though no less authoritarian.

The fact that political role occupancy attracts persons who may not have relevant training, who may place role defence before national interest, who have characteristics associated with authoritarian personalities, must be regarded as a system fault, and appears to be a common feature of all political systems of which we have knowledge. One consequence is that there is a strong tendency to tackle social and political problems within a power framework, by reference to a personal or group ideology, and by means that favour coercion rather than by analytical and consultative processes that seek to resolve problems. It has led to a consensus developing over time that the problems of social organisation are such that no solutions are possible that do not rest on strong leadership and the employment of coercion, of which the state authorities were once supposed to have a legitimised monopoly. This consensus has a firm foundation in classical theory, that held that there were those who had a right to expect obedience and others who had a moral obligation to obey.[3]

Whether or not such a system failure is an inherent feature of political organisation, survival of civilisations probably requires some processes by which its consequences can be offset. Political theory and comparative politics studies have been more concerned with historical and contemporary description than with consideration of system failures and their possible remedies.

It is possible to conceptualise the ideal society in which leadership can be no more than differentiated role behaviour. This is the concept of a small, wholly participatory society in which roles relate to skills or professions and specialities. Leadership roles are limited to the speciality of coordination and procedures of decision-making. The model is that of a town meeting in which a chair person is sought as a matter of convenience, having no powers or leadership role outside this limited procedural role.

Such a model seems not to be applicable to a large political society. The 'consultative' systems that have been tried in China and elsewhere have not eliminated party influence and the emergence of élites. The British parliamentary system was designed to apply the essentials of this model. The Prime Minister is supposed to preside over a Cabinet and to act in this coordinating or chairman role. In Britain the Prime Minister has, by convention, the right to select Cabinet members and, for this reason, has a dominant position. In other parliamentary systems of the British type, Cabinet members are selected by the governing party, thus limiting the power of the Prime Minister. This is the type of check on the power of political leaders than can be built into a system to avoid system fault.

However, the traditional parliamentary system has serious faults, due to the history of the institution, with serious consequences. First, it is undemocratic or inadequately participatory as a consequence of the party system that has evolved. Government is by no more than 50 per cent of the electorate. Furthermore, the mandate given by elections has no bearing on the policies that parties, once elected, follow. Moreover, the tendency in recent years has been for the Prime

Minister to enact a role far beyond that of coordination and the essentials of the differentiated role model. In Britain the right to select the Cabinet has been used to control the specialised functions of ministers and departments, thus introducing a high level of ideology into functional decision-making. This also occurs in the United States. System failures become apparent when a President is likely to be selected from a small number of candidates each of whom must have major financial support, and none of whom is likely to have the specialised skills required for decision-making; not even those skills required to select persons who do have those skills. The tendency, furthermore, has been for the President to by-pass the permanent and professional administration and to adopt policies that are based on ideology rather than on analysis of facts and of behaviour.

That a Prime Minister or President can, within his/her powers, distort the intended role of leadership in this way is itself a system failure, and probably a dangerous one. There is a need for system flexibility that enables leadership to make decisions in special circumstances; but such flexibility, if not checked, may also give rise to leadership behaviour that creates the crises it is then forced to deal with in this authoritarian manner.

In so far as domestic conditions have led to the selection of authoritarian personalities, and in so far as political systems can be manipulated by such personalities, the probability is that relations between the respective states have been adversely affected. As Holsti has argued, 'closed information processes' seem to lead to a 'bad faith model' in decision-making into which there is built-in a cumulative effect.[4]

A spillover of domestic politics into the international system is understandable in this context. Unemployment, due to technological innovation, trade union responses and the hardships that sometimes flow, social unrest in areas of high unemployment and underprivilege, a general sense that something is wrong, give rise, as they did in Germany before the second world war, to a belief that a new and strong leader is required. This is likely to give rise to leadership that advances simple solutions to the complex problems being experienced by the electorate. These simple solutions are accompanied by assurances of a promising future, despite the obvious sacrifices that are implied in the remedies—cuts in welfare services, wage freezes, decreased taxes on higher incomes that impose greater burdens on lower incomes.

Such a leader is almost certainly not suited in a functional sense to the complexities of the domestic situation. The result is likely to be increased problems of a more complex character as infrastructures are destroyed. More importantly, such a leader is unlikely to be relevant to the international system, where simple solutions are usually those of threat and force. In the simplistic terms of an authoritarian leader, there must, in the West, be a direct conflict of interest between capitalism and any other system that has any of the features of communism, even the capitalist-based welfare state. The one is wholly right, the other wholly wrong. There is a missionary urge to redress the wrong. Underlying this move towards conservatism in the West, there is the fear of change towards a more egalitarian system, the fear that oppressive western systems, of which there are many, will give rise to more liberal systems that will favour income and property redistribution and cast doubt on the contemporary relevance of the traditional achieving system. Just as the socialist states feel threatened by the exposure of the weaknesses of socialism, so the West feels threatened by the exposure of the weaknesses of capitalism. Domestic and foreign policies are as one: defence internally and externally of systems, despite their failings.

There are many such influences at play within political systems that ensure a spillover of domestic politics into the international system. A recent history of Vietnam shows the extent to which a President of the United States may be inclined to spend lives in foreign enterprise as a means of culling favour with conservative or anti-communist factions within the political system.[5] Other studies show the way in which interest groups influence policy in their favour, sometimes at great cost to the general interest. These are well known, much published and accepted as part of the democratic process against which have to be set the benefits of such a process.

This is not a study of such system faults. The point is made only that such system faults have far-reaching consequences and the potential to destroy those values which are sought by the system: freedom of information, freedom of expression, law and order, justice and even survival. It can be deduced that arms control negotiations cannot succeed while such system faults persist. No American President or British Prime Minister can be seen to compromise in a stand against communism for fear of losing political support. Fact, reasoning and analysis must be distorted or suppressed. Great international and domestic risks must be taken. Never must mistake or failure be acknowledged. War becomes the lesser of two evils—the greater being the loss of political power.

Commencing with some simple observations regarding authoritative personalities, and the circumstances in which they achieve office, we logically enter into areas of great political complexity. Authoritarian personalities find that in order to deal in their own way with those situations which made it possible for them to come to power in the first instance, they must by-pass the normal state decision-making processes, they must select their own agents, act outside the usual political institutions, rely on a great deal of political deception, and exploit to the full their personal power and position. This raises questions about the institutions of states: whether they are suited to the tasks assigned them, whether government itself is capable of carrying those responsibilities that are traditionally held to be those of the state, in particular responsibilities for foreign affairs.

The problem can be seen in closer perspective when the relationships of factions within states are analysed. In Cyprus, Lebanon, and many other divided nations, power-sharing and agreements on political control seem not to be possible. The problem comes down to who shall occupy what role. Ethnic, religious and tribal groups can be led into conflict very largely as a result of personality factors such as we have been considering.

Later we turn to consider some of the options that are available, some of the ways in which these system failings can be offset. Suffice it at this stage merely to observe the spillover of personalities into international politics.

NOTES

1. See, for example, one of the earliest treatments of this subject, F. Greenstein, *Personality and Politics.*
2. Official statements in relation to the Grenada invasion of 1983 were widely debated from this perspective. There appeared to be in the USA a wide acceptance of 'misinformation' and exclusion of press scrutiny as a norm in the political process. 'Covert' activities were acknowledged as being part of this norm.
3. See Chapter 2 note 2.
4. See Bibliography.
5. See Stanley Karnow, *Vietnam: A history.*

4. Elites and the 'Common Good'

Consideration of authoritarian personalities brings us to the subject of élites generally. Much has been written about power élites, their values, their interest base and the networks they establish. Usually, as with authoritarian personalities, the study of power élites attributes blame or responsibility with the implication that if those concerned were not to behave as they do, the problems created would vanish.

This is wishing away fundamental system features and system faults that are inherent in modern political systems. No blame, in this sense, can be attributed either to persons or élites as a group. They seek to pursue their interests within existing structures and institutions. The structures and institutions that have evolved over time, and the philosophies that have given rise to them, do not require that the individual or group has some duty to promote the general welfare of the society and its members. In the free enterprise system their achievements are supposed to do that. The behaviour that is criticised is precisely that which is supposed to promote the interests of the society and its members. If we were seeking to attach blame, then it would be more reasonable to look to publics that seem to give support to authoritarian personalities and their simplistic solutions, and who envy and respect successful élites. We shall return to this feature later.

Rather than attach blame, we need to look deeper than the behaviour of leaders, élites and publics. Civilisations are in crisis. The nature of this crisis does not need to be spelled-out. Its domestic and international aspects are before us every day. There are a few societies that appear to be stable and few relationships that are cooperative. Modern civilisations are in a transition stage from order based on coercion to an order that is self-sustaining, a transition from positive law and central control to some form of social organisation, the nature of which eludes us, that enables individual development and participatory control. The transition is inevitably a critical stage in evolution and from which civilisation will emerge only if goals are clearly perceived and deliberately pursued. Leadership and élites are a product of what exists, of contemporary stages in growth. In the absence of clear goals and processes towards other forms of social organisation they cannot be expected to lead or to act in ways that are contrary to their immediate interests. In the absence of alternatives, their interests are in maintaining existing structures and institutions in whatever society they happen to be, free enterprise or other.

When steps taken to deal with political, social, economic and security problems fail, when theory and expectations are falsified by experience, when there appear to be no agreed guidelines, when there are not even agreed goals, when there appear to be no answers to problems of survival, it is time to start questioning basic assumptions, even those views and opinions on which there has been, and is still, a wide consensus. If there is a group that is blameworthy in contemporary conditions, then it is scholars, whose responsibility it is to question. They, seeking no less an élite status and acceptance and achievement within their own environments, must be regarded as having failed in this respect. While there are some dissidents within their own specialisations, the great majority of scholars work within paradigms without question, work inductively and seek support for their theses rather than falsification, and avoid abduction and the need to examine their fundamental hypotheses.[1]

The origins of our philosophical assumptions are in the phasing-out of conceptions of civilisation that rested on natural law and a set of god-given rules of conduct. In that ambiguous state there was little scope for questioning, and little call for it. Societies were small, roles were clearer and authority constrained by dependency relationships that were close and direct. Once, however, greater numbers, technological revolutions and power relations influenced structures, interest groups emerged and roles became politically important. Leadership could no longer be confined to differentiated role behaviour. The decision-making function was based on élite value judgements. At this point of evolution a quite fundamental assumption was being introduced into political thought that sharply differentiated modern civilisations from their natural law beginnings. The assumption was that politics was concerned with the authoritative allocation of values rather than an allocation that emerged out of a face-to-face interaction of dependencies. There were no givens, no ultimate truths, no goals outside those that were the end-product of the now free decision-making of élites.[2]

There being no rules, no stated goals, it was necessary to introduce the notion of the 'common good'. This provided a legitimised goal for decision-makers, while still leaving them total freedom of decision-making. It was for them to decide what was the balance between the requirements of society as a whole and the pursued interests of its individual members. In this sense, structures and institutions became the dominant interest. The individual had to be socialised into them, rather than they meet the needs of the individual.

There was no sudden change from one thought system to the other. Natural law beliefs persisted and were incorporated into authoritative decision-making through canon law, ultimately giving added legitimacy and even sanctity to élite decision-making. Yet there was, potentially, a dramatic shift in thought, the full significance of which we are only now beginning to comprehend. The nature of the shift can best be appreciated by comparing western political thinking and decision-making today with political thought and decision-making in the Islamic world.[3]

The freedom to decide political issues, guided only by some remnants of natural law, immediately raised problems of decision-making that have tormented political philosophers ever since. Whose role is it to make value judgements? How are decision-makers to be selected? How are they to be controlled so that the common good prevails? How is this common good to be determined and defined? To what extent, and in what ways, are subjects to be consulted? Hence the interest in the notion of democracy.

The concept of democracy that was relevant once natural law norms were subject to élite decision-making, implied small, even face-to-face societies in which there could be effective participation and consultation. In practice modern societies are complex, and meaningful political participation is impossible. Representation, in some form or another, is the best that can be hoped for.

Once there was a need for representative rather than consensus government, adversary institutions developed and powerful decision-making élites emerged. They were those who over the years and through the processes of development from primitive to industrial societies had accumulated capital, had educational advantages, had obtained leadership roles and could exercise influence over communications and in one way or another had a position of power and influence. It would have been surprising if such élites did not interest themselves in the political process, either through a desire to exercise decision-making power, or to ensure that the political system continued to serve their special interests. It was inevitable that there would emerge a system in which an authoritative allocation of resources and values was made by a small minority whose values were not necessarily those that related to the common good. Once there was a departure from given rules of conduct as prevailed under primitive natural law thinking, once there was freedom of decision-making, there were inevitably struggles for the power of decision-making. Leadership was no longer differentiated role behaviour: it carried with it power to control and to decide. There was a parallel struggle to ensure that decision-makers were constrained in the making of their value judgements. It is for these reasons that western political philosophy has been so much concerned with notions of morality, ethics, justice and freedom. It is for this reason, also, that modern societies are challenging the roles and nature of central authorities.

It is the constraints on decision-making that have failed and been seen to fail. The appeals for law and order, and constitutional government that observes the political norms that have evolved over time, no longer disguise the conflict been élite interests and the needs of the individual. There is generally an erosion of authority and defensive responses by authorities. Decision-makers are not being perceived as being concerned with the common good,[4] and this gives rise to dissent, revolutionary changes in leadership and systems, individual frustrations and local violence. This has, in turn, led to even more coercion in an endeavour to enforce law and order to preserve structures and institutions. In the domestic and in the international spheres, there appears to be no way out of this vicious circle. Civilisations are threatened.

Let us question the original hypotheses—that there can be no givens, that politics must be based on value allocations by authoritative élites. Let us hypothesise, on the contrary, that natural law, even God-given laws—as is the case in Islamic thought—serve as a guide to decision-making. However, let us modify this belief to the extent that contemporary scientific knowledge makes this possible. Let us hypothesise, in the place of God-given laws, the existence of certain ontological human needs. These are not 'rights' to be accorded by a paternalistic authority, but needs in the sense that the human organism *will* and *must* pursue them, acting alone or in association with others, regardless of consequences to self and to society. These are the kinds of physical and social needs hypothesised by Maslow and others. They are universal, ontological, part of the development process of the individual. They include such personal and social needs as a need for stimulus, security, identity, recognition and distributive justice.[5] If we assume this, then a quite different political philosophy evolves. The common good is determined, not by value judgements, not by authoratitive allocations of resources, but by reference to these needs and means by which they are pursued. Let us assume that such needs can be defined precisely so that they give to decision-makers an adequate and unambiguous framework in which to determine resource distribution and policies generally.

In such a pure form there would be no need for any consideration of all those conceptual notions that have bothered political philosophers in the value judgement model. Politics would not be interesting for interest groups and élites! Democracy would not be an issue, for policy-making would be no more than role differentiation: there would be those who were public servants and who administered the political system according to predetermined goals and rules, deduced from a needs theory. There would be no power or advantage attached to decision-making. There would be no politics, no authoritative allocation of resources, that reflected value judgements. There would be no anxieties about system types and how representatives were selected. Considerations of freedom, ethics and justice would be irrelevant: they would be built into decision-making automatically as human needs were pursued.

Sibley has used such a model to argue that 'politics both reflects the generally rapid departure from primitive human nature and in turn contributes to the widespread uncertainty about possibilities of deliberately guiding man's collective life'.[6] 'While there is value attached to man's potential to create his own order, the result of his free decision-making, no longer constrained by any given laws, had led to despotic regimes and threats to civilization.'[7] 'The explanation is that most political authority is only partly "authoritative" or legitimized, the other part being corrupted by special interests and piratical elements.'[8]

This pure-type Brave New World is very different from Huxley's model, which imposed order from the top, be it in some ways a benevolent order. The needs model derives its structures from the human needs of its members. It is not persons that determine structures and policies, but their ontological needs, which as individuals, they may not be fully aware of. It is an order that places the needs of the individual in supreme control. The common good does not stem from a compromise between the social good—defined by interests groups that exercise political power—and the interests of the individual. There is no social good outside the human needs of the members of society as individuals.

This model raises sharply the question whether defence of structures, institutions and societies can remain the main concern of policies, or whether the main goal will inevitably be the pursuit of the needs of the individual members of society. The old notion of the common good, the meshing of the general interest with the individual interest, the seeking of a balance between the two, effectively dodged the issue. The argument was that the balance was one that gave the best to the most. This balance could be determined only within the value system of representative decision-makers, and therefore, was, and had to be, an ideological phenomenon. As élite structures, by definition, provide the ideal balance within any existing ideological framework, they must be enforced and defended by constraints on the individual. If necessary they must be defended by constraints on the majority of individuals, as in South Africa, for, again by definition, ideology is a better guide to the common good than the perceived and expressed judgement of the majority. In this thought system the individual is infinitely malleable. He/she can and is required to fit into the ideologically-based system, because this is the system best suited to his/her needs in the view of power élites.

The alternative model, that focuses on the individual and his ontological needs, suggests that this approach to the management of political systems must ultimately fail. Structures are required to be modified to meet human needs. If not they will not be stable and societies will be disrupted. There is no longer credibility in the rationalisations put forward to justify the concept of the common good or the balance between social and individual interests. The individual is finally winning the battle—at great cost to himself and to societies.

The clear signal is a need for change processes, means by which failed systems can move toward altered forms in a deliberate and planned manner. The change processes needed are those that enable all concerned to analyse their needs and interests and to determine the basic features of structures sought. The need is for processes of discovery, not arbitrary interests and simplistic behavioural notions.

As will be observed later, western philosophy and experience is rich in structure maintenance. It is weak on theories and practices of change outside spasmodic change by violence.

NOTES

1. The Kuhn-Popper debates of the early 1960s had an important influence on political thinking. But because they took place within the general field of philosophy, they did not have a significant impact on teaching and research in the field of international politics. Furthermore, the emphasis that Popper placed on falsification made the issue seem irrelevant to international studies where propositions cannot readily be falsified. Only more recently has attention been given to the work of Peirce, who was rarely referred to during this debate. See Burton, *Dear Survivors*, pp. 95-9, for further comments.
2. See the opening chapters of Brecht, *Political Theory*, for a clear exposition of this problem.
3. The report, *Crisis in Muslim Education* by Husain and Ashraf, is a most instructive document from this point of view. It has not been possible to do justice to the significance of the Islamic issue for world politics in this study. Within the next decade it will be a major issue in world politics. Much depends on how the seeming conflict between Islamic thought and western cultural values will be resolved. One of the practical difficulties is that western culture is perceived by Islamic thinkers and politicians as being traditional culture that attaches prime importance to structures. The needs approach that is emerging may form a bridge that could avoid conflict in the future.
4. See Huber and Form, Wright, and Sibley.
5. The important contribution has been by Sites, to whom many references are made later in this study.

6. See p. 37.
7. See p. 45.
8. See p. 94.

5. Deviance and Dissent

In our anxiety never to attribute problems of behaviour to the systems we seek to preserve, deviance of all kinds has traditionally been defined by reference to social norms and not to individual needs. In other words, behaviour by members of society that is against the accepted social norms has been treated as a fault in the individual or group so deviating. It has been held to be due to a failure on the part of the individual to respond to the socialisation process, or alternatively to some abnormal mental state. On this basis it was logical to develop political theories that asserted the monopoly and legitimised use of force by authorities over minorities, designed to maintain law and order and the norms of society in the interests of the majority. It can be deduced from this that authorities have a right ot command and that others have a moral obligation to obey.[1] There are logical extensions to this position, for example, the notions of majority rule and of democracy even as applied to multiethnic societies or class societies in which minorities are likely to be disfranchised permanently.

A fundamental behavioural question is raised by such a political philosophy: To what extent can the individual, whose ontological needs must be met, be socialised into conforming behaviour that is incompatible with the pursuit of such needs? More recent thinking suggests that this emphasis on socialisation cannot be justified in behavioural terms.[2] A second issue is whether any authority has a right to impose its value systems on minorities. By right, in this connection, is meant ability or power over the longer term.

In recent sociological studies deviance has been treated as a function of labelling: behaviour that societies label as deviant, the labels being the formal descriptions that arise out of the articulation of social norms.[3] This approach has the advantage that it brings to our attention the probability of instances in which there is conflict between the norms of society and how they are applied on the one hand, and the legitimate interests and human needs of the individual on the other.

These two approaches raise the question whether society or the individual is the independent variable. Do societies emerge as a result of a systematic process that is inherent in social organisation? Must its members, therefore be socialised into conformity with evolving social structures? Or do societies evolve as a result of a struggle by individuals to create environments that will ensure that their human needs are satisfied?

Such questions pose a challenge to the foundations of political theories of both the Right and the Left. They threaten to bring about a paradigm shift in the course of which most of the underlying assumptions of political theory and traditional policies will be challenged. It is the kind of re-examination that creates adversary politics within academic institutions and political strife in society as a whole as the contending approaches join battle. It is a re-examination that has international implications no less challenging than the domestic ones. If the explanation of deviance rests on an understanding of the individual as the unit member of the national society, it can be deduced that the explanation of aggression at the international level is also in the frustration of the nation that finds itself confronting the norms of the international system.

During this century the separate disciplines have concerned themselves with their own subject matters. To a very large extent, understandably, they have adopted the same set of philosophical and political assumptions. However, each is running into trouble: each is encountering problems in the sense that experience seems to contradict theory. Hidden in the mass of contemporary interdisciplinary literature is another philosophy, one that takes the individual, as the unit of explanation [4]. It attaches importance to the individual, not for reasons of value preference, but because this is being found to be the only way in which to resolve the intellectual problems of explanation. Political theory is still taught at universities as though it stopped with Marx. Students are led to deduce that there had been no political theory development in the twentieth century. It is arguable, on the contrary, that there has been far more fundamental thinking on issues since the 1950s than in all previous history of thought. Now in the 1980s there is a reasonable doubt about the fundamental classical assumption that structure is the independent variable. Sociology, law, anthropology, sociobiology and, indeed, all disciplines are now providing evidence of this growing uncertainty. The individual is more and more being found to be, not the invented one, convenient to the particular theories of economists, political theorists and lawyers, but a being who has certain potentialities that will be pursued, regardless of the consequences to society and self.

However, as is usually the case with a shift in thinking, there are many questions raised that need to be dealt with satisfactorily before there can be a commitment to a new model. What is the relationship between human needs, if they exist in this universal and genetic form, and culture? What is the time factor involved in the alteration of societies to bring them into conformity with human needs? Is there any evidence of historical trends that are more than empirically and ideologically inspired observations? Is there evidence that the pressures of individuals in the pursuit of whatever interests and needs there are can overcome the coercive pressures of structures and authorities that dominate them? Can the alternative hypothesis explain what the original one explained, and more beside? Does it answer unanswered questions? Is the human needs hypothesis supported by empirical evidence in biology and related areas of study?

It is only when these questions are resolved that any clear meaning can be given to the term deviance. Either the notion relates to the individual and his behaviour that is out of step with social norms, or the notion relates to the authorities and interests that are responsible for the creation and maintenance of structures and norms that are at variance with the human needs of the individual. Which is the independent variable that finally controls the norms and the systems of society? Is a synthesis possible? Is there such a phenomenon as genetic culture? And can genetic-cultural needs be identified? While both structures and needs require analysis, while both must be the units of analysis, which is the unit of explanation? Is it possible that the notion of deviance is meaningful only when it is applied to authorities and interest groups responsible for the environmental conditions that force unit members of societies to break with the norms of their society and pursue their needs by other means? Have we failed to define and to explain deviance because we have attributed the behaviour we are endeavouring to describe to the wrong partner in the authority-individual relationship? These are questions that are relevant to socialist systems as much as to the capitalist. Socialism solves some problems, but it has not solved the problems of participation, alienation, boredom and the need to repress the symptoms of these.

It has already been implied that the clarification of the notion of deviance is not just an intellectual exercise. The notion goes to the heart of public policy and to consideration of the nature of the state. Indeed, it is of even greater significance, for it goes to the heart also of industrial, family and classroom relations, and all social relationships in which decision-making roles are enacted. It raises issues of equality of opportunities for development and of participation. A consideration of deviance involves a total social theory. One test of a social theory is, in practice, whether it clarifies the notion of deviance.

The question what the nature of deviance is is probably at the heart of most of our relationship problems: who is right and who is wrong, who is at fault, or is there no one at fault; are we not dealing with problems of structure and conflicts of interest that arise out of the structure. Our international problems appear to have national origins, in particular, origins in institutions and structures that are incompatible with human needs. Domestic failures are attributed to alien influences. This is not surprising. Relationship problems generally stem from the problems of the parties concerned. It is their insecurities, their inability to change and to adapt, their conventions and behavioural habits, their projections and distorted perceptions, that are at the root of problems of relationships. When President Reagan communicated to the joint Houses of the Commons and Lords in Britain in 1982 his desire to 'liberate' Soviet citizens, what was it he was going to liberate them from—unemployment, street mugging, inequalities of opportunity, race riots, highly organised crime and political corruption and policies designed to promote party political advantages? Or was he projecting his concerns about the system for which he had assumed responsibility?

Dissent and deviance, whether at the domestic or the international level, are symptoms of problems, manifestations of conflicts between human needs and aspirations and the structures and institutions that determine the environments of the individual or nation. Finally, it is the latter that must adjust to the former: social structures are there to serve the needs of members of society, not the other way about.

The same must be said of terrorism. It is a symptom of a problem. Behind the terrorist is a community of feeling and a support group. Reprisals and punishments merely create an increased sense of frustration and injustice. Today's terrorists are tomorrow's national leaders. Labels such as deviant, dissident, terrorist, revolutionary and rebel may reasonably apply to emotionally disturbed individuals who need sympathetic treatment and even control. No less they may be labels that apply to progressive and concerned leadership of peoples who have legitimate goals to pursue. It is important to differentiate between the two. Labelling is usually dysfunctional and a defensive device used for political purposes.

NOTES

1. This phrase, taken from Lloyd as already noted, has been used frequently. Within the paradigm that is emerging which attaches importance to human needs of identity and control, this traditional notion is at the heart of the problems of law and order. The repetition is to stress this challenge to traditional thought that is emerging.

2. Sites has drawn attention to the over-emphasis that has been given to socialisation as a control process. It is the needs factor that is not taken adequately into account in explaining deviance. It is because the individual seeks that control necessary to pursue human needs that the notion of 'rights to expect obedience' is challenged in social life. It should be noted that the same argument applies at the international level: greater powers have limited abilities, despite their superior power, to control the behaviour of smaller states and nationalities.

3. This issue of labelling is well dealt with by Box.

4. See Chapter 15 for references, and an outline of this thinking.

6. Recession or *Un*development?

We are strangely devoid of any explanation as to why private enterprise societies have increasingly experienced problems of crime and violence. There are simplistic explanations, such as the breakdown of the family unit, and a lessened respect for authority. These explanations counsel firmer and more conservative policies in the home, at school, in the streets and at the level of central government. Similarly, there are no adequate explanations of poverty, especially in the more affluent societies. The simplistic explanation is that there is individual under achievement for reasons of personal will and ability. This counsels limitations on support or assistance, even punishment. The problem is not defined as a system fault: it is a personal fault.

The empirical data on crime and poverty can be interpreted in ways that support the conservative ideology that places responsibility on the individual, or the liberal ideology that attributes responsibility to the economic and social system. Whatever the explanation, the fact remains that within the private enterprise system as now managed in western economies there are high and increasing levels of crime and poverty.

Similarly, there is no adequate explanation of unemployment. Some unemployment is due clearly to the dynamics of the economic system and the mobility of labour. Higher levels of unemployment may, at times, be due to increased levels of technological change and immobility of labour. However, developed western economies now experience long-term unemployment at high levels. The social and political consequences are far-reaching. There does appear to be a connection between crime, poverty and unemployment.

The need to defend the institutions of the private enterprise system requires that a blind eye be turned to its system defects. These simplistic explanations of crime, poverty and unemployment are the turning of a blind eye: there is a great reluctance on the part of politicians and professional economists to ask questions about recession, the answers to which would cast doubt on the stability and future of the private enterprise system as it is now being managed.

This cultural or interested orientation has grave international implications. It is the long-term health of the private enterprise system as now managed that socialism is challenging. It is insecurities experienced about this system that lead western political leaders to be so defensive of it, and so aggressive against alternatives that emerge in other countries within their own spheres of influence. The movement away from the welfare state and away from attempts to manage the system to ensure greater welfare—whether problems were due to structures or to individual weaknesses—has had serious international consequences. It has made developed western nations more fearful and defensive.

This self-delusion about the health of the contemporary private enterprise system leads to a belief that those who live in communist societies are, by comparison, far worse-off in their style of life, seek to get 'liberated', and would respond favourably to western intervention. It is quite clear that there is a far higher proportion of persons in developed western societies who enjoy a high quality of life, with an appreciation of the arts, with opportunities for higher education and travel, and with jobs that are pleasant. It is also clear that in western developed societies there are up to 10 per cent of people on average unemployed, and up to twice that figure of unemployment amongst minority ethnic populations. They have no recognised social role, no identity in the economic system, and feel alienated and insecure. Employment, old age support, health and education are not a cause for a sense of insecurity in communist countries. Furthermore, the communist states are developing states. Living standards are on the increase. It is probably a false assumption that there is no overwhelming support for the communist system in those countries in which it has now taken root. It may be a delusion that peoples in developing countries within the western sphere of influence favour the free enterprise system as a means of overcoming their feudalism and poverty.

It behoves us, therefore, to acknowledge system faults that create international insecurities and to seek explanations of them and ways in which they can be overcome, either by system change or by system management. Neither monetary nor protectionist policies have been effective in dealing with unemployment. It can no longer be treated as an acceptable institution of the system because of its domestic and inter-national implications. The simplistic explanations, while they serve a party-political function, now have to be challenged in the broader national and global interest.

There are both theoretical and empirical reasons for believing that what western economies have been experi-encing are not recessions, but *un*development, that is, a condition in which there are increasing inequalities of incomes, reductions in the rate of growth, increasing poverty, the run-down of infrastructures and a decline in the educational, health and other welfare services associated with development, to the point at which previously developed systems take on the features of an underdeveloped economy.

Great Britain already has these features of *un*development. Despite the discovery of oil, which should have been a major boost to the economy, unemployment has persisted, in spite of the growing needs for the maintenance of infrastructures, educational and health establishments and services, housing and other demands on labour. —The rich have throughout maintained or improved their position while the poor have become poorer. The United States is beginning to feature the same trends. In both cases defence budgets have been maintained or increased. The question that suggests itsself is whether the internal insecurities have promoted an external fear, whether unemployment is a system fault that cannot be remedied without a fundamental change in economic and political structures, or whether it is, as argued, merely a cyclical phenomenon or a temporary consequence of technological development.

There is one option that has not featured in economic advice, namely, policies designed to promote stability by greater continuity in demand through greater equality of income. It may be that such an option does not provide an answer to the problem. This we shall examine. It may also be that there are reasons for not examining such an option.

a cynical view is that economists are no different from other interest groups. They are educated in and enjoy the privileges of societies which are typically characterised by gross inequalities in opportunities. It can be understood why they should, as a group, avoid options that would destroy such inequality and privilege. They do not experience directly the political and social consequences of inequality.

More importantly, economists inevitably serve established interests, especially economists at the traditional centre of learning. As advisers, they are not in a position to change structures and institutions, they advise within those that exist. Economists within a capitalist system give certain advice, and those within a socialist system give different advice in respect of similar problems. The advice given to conservative governments in the West is different from the advice given to liberal governments. Joan Robinson once observed,

Economics itself . . . has always been partly a vehicle for the ruling ideology of each period. . . .

It is the business of the economists, not to tell us what to do, but to show why what we are doing anyway is in accord with proper principles. Certainly, there seems currently to be a strong tendency for professional advisers to governments in the western economies to justify, on economic grounds, whatt the political parties in power would wish to do anyway.[1]

In recent years, both in the UK and USA, economic and financial policies have happened to be those which businessmen and others who have supported the governments in office, would wish to see—policies that have led to reductions in expenditure on social services accompanied by more regressive taxation. These have been recommended by economists acting professionally. It does not follow that these policies are necessarily destructive of the interests of the bulk of the population and of the economy generally. There are many arguments for and against. However, it does seem to be more than coincidence that the policies and interests of intellectual and political élites do, in practice, coincide.

However, there are explanations for western policies that go beyond such intellectual corruption. Economists and politicians have been preoccupied with problems of unemployment, inflation, the balance of payments and others that require immediate solutions or, if not solutions, immediate control. They have not been able to maintain a wider and longer-term perspective. They have been in roles that inhibit consideration of past and future developments and consequences. Indeed, despite the titles given to books and articles such as Keynes', which claimed to be a 'general theory',[2] it can reasonably be argued that economic theorising, in any historical and dynamic sense, ceased with the onset of the Great Depression of the 1930s.From then on economists increasingly focused on the immediate political issues: unemployment before the war, wartime problems of production and control, post-war reconstruction, international trade and aid to developing economies, problems of the welfare state, exchange control and balance of payments, inflation and stagnation.

For these purposes models were invented that conformed with the social and political climate. They were models of the free enterprise system and its institutions and of monopolistic competition. All reflected assumptions and value judgements that were social and political in characte, and not derived from, or justified by, any economic theory or analysis. Economic theory and analysis was, rather, built onto them. There were assumptions made about the need for incentives. These had favourable tax consequences for higher income groups; but the assumption of incenttives, and the different forms they could take if they were required, were never subjected to psychological or empirical investigation. There were assertions about the inevitability of, and even the social need for, inequalities of income, as for example the claim that the arts would not prosper in an egalitarian society. There were assumptions made about the economies of scale which suited some investment prospects in the short term, but which took no account of the participatory problems that occur in large enterprises. There were assumptions about the nature of 'economic man', and his dominant interest in the acquisition of material goods that made irrelevant considerations of participation, recognition and identity. These he could ursue outside the workplace. Joan Robinson was fully justified in stressing the influence of ideology on economists.

A knowledge base existed in sociology, psychology, anthropology and politics, as well as in economics itself; but it was not articulated and made part of the consensual thinking sufficiently to offset political and élite value judgements. In particular, economists seem to have lost sight of the dynamics of the processes of development within which occur all the particular and immediate problems that have attracted their attention. They have lost sight of process and general theory, not because history and general theory are not amongst the tools that are available to them, it is just that they have not been used, so preoccupied have economists been with their ideologies and with that which is politically immediate. Western economics, which forms the bulk of economic thinking, has become the study of how to make the best use of scarce resources in a particular type of system and, furthermore, at a particular stage of its development. It has been removed from the dynamics of economic development that are common to all systems. The current problems, which are the preoccupation of economists, have not been, and are not being, analysed within such a dynamic or historical framework.

Even the study of developing economies has usually been made within the framework used for developed ones. They have been studied as though they were at the disposal of the developed economies. Policies and pressures have been applied that have not been appropriate and have led to the destruction of socially important infrastructures. Social values are also economic goods to be conserved and consumed.

If there had been analyses made of economies that are still developing and in transition from one stage to another, different types of questions and different approaches would have been in evidence. If such a dynamic approach to development could be recaptured, then it might be possible to examine current problems within developed economies from a different point of view, and to ask different and more rewarding questions relating to the particular and immediate problems economists are dealing with.

Currently, we are given to believe that technologies have created conditions in which there must be longer-term and even continuing unemployment: 'recession' is to be permanent. We are told that we have more labour resources than society requires. We have to plan for leisure and for idleness. But the same arguments were used in the 1930s. Late in 1930 a prominent US banker was reported as saying:

If there has been a recession, is it not because the nation has achieved and produced on a scale so large that there has been thrust upon us the necessity of pausing? . . . It is a glorious thing to contemplate that, as a nation, we have too much rather than too little.[3]

The author of *The New Dealers* said, 'The New Deal was necessary. It was caused by one simple fact: that we can produce more than enough for everybody in this country. This is something new in human history.'[4] It was probably new, also, to some millions then out of work and short of essential requirements. Meantime, re-employment remained the priority policy. Little wonder that it did not matter during the Depression what the re-employed were employed to do. The contemporary equivalent is voluntary social work or youth employment and training programmes that have no prospect of leading to relevant occupations.

Within the context of development, *unemployed resources that are made available as the result of techonological development, must be regarded as a valued asset.* They provide society with an opportunity to undertake the production of goods and services for home and foreign consumption which it was not previously able to afford. Technological development has progressively led to more and more manpower and capital being diverted into defence and defence industries on a scale that previously could not be afforded. One of the questions to be asked is why this is so. Why was the diversion not into goods and services required by the consumers generally, such as education, health and others?—which, in fact, have been cut down because the economies cannot afford them! Was it really a need for defence, or was it because of a political unwillingness to enter into a system that undertakes the provision of required goods and services on the basis of need rather than ability to acquire? Was the 'defence' a defence against a trend in world society toward such a system, dubbed for convenience socialist or communist?

In value terms this view is understandable. Indeed, in value terms there can be no argument against élites seeking to preserve those systems that meet their needs. However, it could also be that the preservation of some values is finally destructive of more fundamental ones. Attempts to solve an economic problem such as unemployment, or attempts to control inflation, within a framework that did not take into account wider social concerns and the need for adequate educational and health infrastructures could force just those more fundamental structural changes that the policies were designed to prevent.

Let us examine this probability more closely. Implicit in the traditional belief is that economic systems are in a constant process of development, except in so far as there is a temporary pause or halt in the process from time to time. The reason for such temporary changes in the rate of development may be due, in this view, to a variety of market and extra-market causes: technological innovations and investments, altering policies by cartels, wars, and all other factors that affect economies. The development process, however, is assumed to continue. These fluctuations are regarded as an inevitable and uncomfortable part of it. Financial and monetary policies, not structural changes, are regarded as the cure.

An alternative view is that recession and depression are evidence not of fluctuations in development, but of regression, that is, *un*development. There is no reason to believe that system processes continue indefinitely in the same direction. The development process can have within it the potential for *un*development, as when fermentation increases yeast at an accelerating rate until the point is reached at which, as the result of fermentation, the yeast is killed.

A synthesis of these two theories may be possible. For instance, it may be that temporary conditions trigger recession, and that the policies adopted to deal with this set into motion an *un*developed process. Once set in motion such a process could have its own systemic mechanisms in the absence of any correcting policies.

If there are built-in mechanisms in the developmental process that can reverse the process, or if short-term policies trigger regressive systemic processes, it can be deduced that as the developmental process proceeds, the extent and duration of the recession will become greater. Permanent unemployment on an extensive scale would be a likely feature at advanced stages. The ability of the economy to provide the educational and other requirements for its own existence could be seriously impaired, rendering the economy unable to deal with competition from other systems. Having in mind that economic conditions affect social and political conditions, it could be deduced that a stage would be reached when societies would be disrupted beyond the possibility of re-establishment in their previous form.

At an empirical level, it is reasonable to advance the following tentative thesis. The development process consists of a progressive change from agriculture and other primary industries towards more specialisation and industrialisation, and then, from this secondary stage, to the service or tertiary stage of development. There appears to be a fourth stage. The process of development creates within each of these three sectors of the economy, and between them, marked inequalities in skills, opportunities and incomes. These inequalities have far-reaching market consequences that promote structural distortions in the system. The fourth stage is when these distortions are corrected, thus maintaining a stable demand for the products of the first three sectors. This stage has not been entered in existing developed economies. The reason is that at an advanced point in the third stage, decision-making comes within the control of those whom the developmental process favours and who resist any correction to the inequalities that the developmental process created.

In order to determine whether we experience recession or *un*development, whether this empirical view is valid and, if so, whether the process is a systemic one or a result of policy, it is necessary to be clear on the nature of the developmental process itself.

The developmental process has taken, in our twentieth century experience, two forms. There has been the 'natural' process through the primary, secondary and tertiary stages, which was the experience of the currently developed states. It was a continuous process in which the developments in one sector paved the way for developments in subsequent sectors. It was the experience of the USA, Canada, Australia and New Zealand, amongst others. There has also been a 'forced' process whereby industrialisation has been introduced in the absence of the full development of the primary sector. This has taken place in international conditions of colonialism, investment by international corporations, and other conditions that have rendered the economies concerned in a mixed state of development and underdevelopment. The social and political structures are those that would follow from such a mix. The so-called 'developing' economies are, as a consequence, under developed in their important agricultural sector and likely to remain so in the absence of a planned programme designed to recreate the process. This is technically difficult and politically unlikely in the absence of a political revolution. Problems of rural poverty, seasonal famine, inadequate or non-existent educational and health services, rural population, drift to cities, and conspicuous inequalities persist.

An analysis of the 'natural' developmental process as experienced by developed states should throw light not only on that process, but also on the nature of the problem being faced by the underdeveloped economies.

Unlike the contemporary underdeveloped economies, the developed ones commenced their development on a strong agricultural base. Political power resided in the land. Capital investment and the first steps toward industrialisation were associated with agriculture. Indeed, the resistance to industrial development outside the requirements of primary production retarded such development. Arguments in favour of assisted industrialisation were opposed by arguments in favour of 'balanced economies'. A committee set up by the Australian government produced *The Australian Tariff* in 1927. It stated,

'It is felt that a country is inferior in status if it does not have the industries of advanced countries, and that for Australia to be mainly dependent on primary industries would be to place its people in the position of 'hewers of wood and drawers of water' for the people of more favoured countries.[5]

On the other hand, the Empire Economic Union asserted in 1939 that

Any economic policy which is based, not upon immediate individual interest, but upon the conception of national co-operation, and which aims at establishing a proper balance between the various elements in production. . . must include, as a principal object, the maintenance of a successful agriculture and of a prosperous agricultural population.[6]

Both sides sought reasons to support their case. In favour of primary production there were arguments that related to national security, to comparative costs and to political stability. In favour of industrialisation there were arguments in favour of self-sufficiency, employment opportunities, cultural development and protection of infant industries. The dangers of relying on exports that were constantly in surplus supply, such as wheat, were emphasised. The different arguments gave rise to policies of protection for one section of the economy or the other. The arguments were designed to favour particular productive structures, not the interests of consumers. However, the result over the years of development appears to be movements from a firm base of primary production to related forms of industrialisation and to further development within a conservative political framework that tended to favour consolidation of existing structures before cautious innovations.

The end-product of the conflict between the contending interests was a gradual process, no great and sudden drift to cities leading to rural poverty, and no conspicuous structural unemployment despite the changes that were taking place. Wartime conditions in Europe accelerated the process in the New World and brought the arguments to a close. Whereas in the early stages industry, protected by tariffs and subsidies, was regarded as a burden on agriculture, secondary industry, once established, provided an increasing demand for agricultural products. The income redistribution necessary to bring about a shift in productive structures was made possible by tariffs and subsidies. There was no direct tax necessary, such as an income tax.

The empirical evidence of this process is available in statistical form.[7] The same pattern was present in the development of Australia, New Zealand and Canada. Despite the belief that subsidised secondary industries were a burden on the primary, resistances were overcome when it was seen that those employed in the secondary sector provided demand for primary sector products on an increasing scale. Without secondary production there would be less demand for primary products, leading to unemployment, underemployment and poverty in the agricultural sector.

The process from secondary to tertiary is less easy. It cannot be accomplished by protection, it has not been promoted by wartime conditions and it must be by the more direct and obvious means of subsidy. Indeed, in a society

Table 6.1 Exports of United States of America, agricultural and non-agricultural (% of totals of value)

Yearly average	Agricultural products	Non-agricultural products
1896-1900	66.2	33.8
1911-1915	49.7	50.3
1916-1920	42.1	57.9
1921-1925	46.2	53.8
1926-1930	36.1	63.9
1931-1935	36.8	63.2
1936-1938	24.4	75.6

seeking some degree of equality of opportunity and wishing to facilitate the processes of change, health and educational services in particular have to be made available through income redistribution by direct or indirect taxation. The view that such services are a drag on the primary and secondary industries is thus enforced, at least in the view of those whose income is most affected. This is despite the obvious fact that the demand of those engaged in service industries reinforces demand for primary and secondary products, just as secondary industries created demand for primary products. Perhaps contemporary resistance to the development of the service sector, and the preference for unemployment, will in due course be overcome in the same manner and by the same arguments, even though the implications would appear to be a direct redistribution of income in the first instance.

However, in the meantime and not unexpectedly, when there is a recession and reduced demand for any reason, such as technological change or some overseas conditions that reduce the profitability of exports, the reflex action is to reduce expenditure on health, education, infrastructures and services generally. This is, in itself, a first step toward *un*development. The reason given at the time is that there has been an over-development of services, and that the services concerned have developed before the stage of economic development warranted them.

There are theoretical and practical justifications. First, it is argued that reduced taxation and increased incentives promote investment in industrial production. Second, monetary policies are held to be necessary to control inflation in conditions in which there is reduced production yet maintained demand. Third, there is the argument of defence requirements. For all these three reasons, it is argued, there is a need to reduce public expenditure on social services.

There appears, in theory, to be a fourth stage. The dynamic process of development appears to create, inevitably it would seem, conditions that, if not unchecked, reverse the process, leading to *un*development. The process of development creates within and between each of these three sectors of an economy marked inequalities of technical skills, opportunities and income. The reason is that scarcities of skills and professional knowledge lead to progressively higher incomes in the newly emerging occupations.

Inequalities of opportunity and incomes have economic consequences that appear to be cumulative. Inequalities promote demands for goods that are not relevant to the particular stage of the development of the economy. There are goods that are 'luxury' in the context of the stage of development. These are conspicuously present in underdeveloped economies. These goods and services are expensive in terms of the loss of the goods and services that are appropriate to the particular stage of development. Specialised or 'luxury' goods, extravagant private transport, special educational and health services of various kinds, distort the economy away from the structure that would prevail if demand were concentrated on those qualities and kinds of goods and services relevant to that stage of development.

It is also part of our experience that as the developmental process continues into the tertiary stage and creates 'stagflation', the remedies applied tend to be cuts in public expenditure and, if possible, in income tax. These accentuate structural distortions in production even more as the poor become poorer and as the better-off maintain their advantages or get richer, accentuating the demand-supply problem. There are widespread social and political consequences that not only restrict production even more, but also threaten the stability of the social and political systems.

The fourth stage of development occurs, in theory, when these conditions are eliminated by reducing the inequalities created. This is theory only, for we have no experience of this fourth stage. Economies seem not to be able to enter this stage before the regression process begins to take over, leading to *un*development and increased inequalities. Why is this?

The attempt to deal with the inflation problem of the advanced tertiary process by means that create unemployment, even only in the short term, intuitively seems not to be rational. Scarcity of goods and services cannot be remedied by their decreased production. Inflationary policies designed to promote consumer demand do not deal with the underlying structural problems. Despite Keynes, inflation and unemployment can occur together. Intuitively, the remedy for a condition of inflation and unemployment is a redistribution of income such that demand is sustained for goods that, at a particular stage of development, are widely consumed at the average and lower income levels—housing and consumer goods and servives generally—thus promoting employment and production in relation to the main demand sector of the economy. Yet redistribution of income is not a subject that is usually discussed in this connection. Indeed, the remedy that is more usually suggested is reduced income tax, with further demand for 'luxury' production of goods and services, and reduced wages and benefits for those on lower incomes and who provide the effective demand for the goods that are relevant to the stage of development.

Are there some social-structural reasons why income redistribution is not put forward as a possible remedy? Why should this process of development be retarded and reversed? Why is this fourth stage which is necessary to enter and to complete in order to consolidate the previous stages, not attained? The answer seems to lie in the political and social structure of society that is created by the developmental process itself. By the time the tertiary sector has emerged and developed, a 'middle' class or income group has effective control.

This process is shown strikingly in the proportion of unskilled labour in various industrial occupations in Australia in 1933.[8] The relative skills and absence of skills are reflected in equalities of income. [9]

Direct and progressive taxation and redistribution of income are resisted by the élite minority that controls the developed economic, social and political systems. The values

Table 6.2

Occupation	Labourers (male) and other wholly unskilled workers %
Fishing & trapping	85.0
Mining & quarrying	63.0
Tobacco growing & manufacture	52.0
Agriculture & dairy farming	45.0
Fibrous materials & textiles	36.0
Manufacture of animal & vegetable products	22.0
Building & construction	14.0
Sports & recreation	10.0
Shipbuilding	3.4
Clothing	2.8
Commerce & trading	1.2
Manufacture of musical and scientific instruments	0.7
Finance	0.7
Public administration & the professions	0.2

of this élite become consensual norms by reason of the fact that this same élite controls the whole socialisation apparatus, including the mass media, education and decision-making—and also the tasks of economic research and advice. Values are attached to 'initiative', 'enterprise' and

Table 6.3

Industrial classification	% employed receiving more than £260 p.a.
Agriculture, pastoral & dairy farming	1.3
Fishing & trapping	2.7
Manufacture : non-metal & furniture	5.3
Manufacture : animal & vegetable products	7.2
Founding, engineering & metal working	8.2
Stone, clay & glass work	10.4
Manufacture : rubber & leather goods	10.5
Mining & quarrying	12.0
Manufacture of foodstuffs	17.1
Commerce	17.6
Manufacture of chemicals, dyes, etc.	19.8
Defence	20.0
Gas, water, electricity	22.6
Health	23.1
Air transport	29.6
Religion	37.9
Property & finance	46.7
Education	50.6
Law & order	52.1
Public administration	55.7

'rewards'. Anti-assistance sentiments are generated against the unemployed, the sick and the aged. Trade unions are influenced by these middle-class and income attitudes and strong 'right'-wing trends emerge throughout the political and social systems. The process is self-generating, and the rich get richer and the poor poorer as a result of the tax and public expenditure policies that are followed. Private health and educational services flourish, while public health and educational services deteriorate. The growing inequalities not only lead to increasingly decreased demand throughout the economy, but also to increased crime, social unrest and political frustration.

There is here a problem of 'social goods'. Elites and others desire a stable and progressive economic and social system, a satisfied population and legitimised authorities. However, it is in the interests of the individual in the élite or controlling group to maintain his/her position of privilege, to resist income redistribution and wider political participation, hoping that sufficient numbers of others in the élite group will make the necessary sacrifices. The social good and the individual good are incompatible. In due course, sufficient of the élite group to destroy the system pursue their individual interests.

These value systems and attitudes become more widespread and more entrenched as incomes increase and as privilege becomes more widespread. There are systemic reinforcements in addition. The more cuts are made in social services, the less efficient are public services and the more attractive become the private services only in the range of higher incomes. Adequate educational, cultural and health services become the property of the few, public transport and infrastructures are neglected. The society takes on the characteristics of an underdeveloped economy.

It follows that, in the absence of some unusual leadership that manages to redress the balance, one of two situations must emerge: either the underprivileged in employment, the socially deprived, become permanently disadvantaged and contained by law and order processes; or there is political unrest and change. For reasons we discuss later, the latter is the more probable.

So far, we have been concerned with the *un*development of the domestic system. The same process of development and the same built-in conditions of *un*development are also present in the international system. There are within the international system the same market inequalities that effectively limit demand for the production of goods and services from the developed states, the same political responses and the same conflict between those who benefit from the system and those who do not. There is the same reluctance to make any income redistribution by any means. Indeed, one of the features of the advanced tertiary process and the reversal of the developmental process, is a reduction not an increase in foreign aid, even with increased GNP, just as it is to reduce benefits in the domestic system.

The developmental process within the international system creates its own tensions between the haves and have nots. Added to this, there are the sharp divisions caused by different political philosophies and systems. Any political movements anywhere in the world, in small or large states, towards greater equality or increased political participation are likely to be regarded by one great power or the other as a threat to its own system. Resistance to feudalism in Central America or to authoritarianism in Eastern Europe are likely to present a challenge to the one system or to the other. Rather than attribute the resistance to system failure, the tendency is to attribute dissent and opposition to external intervention.

These are the conditions that create national insecurity and international suspicion. They justify arms programmes. The same arms programmes, thus justified, also become a means of re-employment and bring to the public's attention in a vivid way the existence of an external enemy. The Coser proposition, that external threat brings internal cohesion, seems to be validated. The defence budget is one area of public expenditure that governments are able to maintain even in recession.

Competition between opposing political systems becomes intense as each tries to undermine further the already weakened system of the other. Each is self-confident that its internal cohesion is superior. Finally, owing to miscalculations about resources and will, one side or the other feels that it has nothing to lose by taking action against the alleged external source of its problem.

The question that is finally posed is whether failure to reach the fourth stage of development is due to system failure or to system management. The same question could be asked in relation to contemporary socialism. Is it socialism that has created fundamental human and production problems, or the management of socialism? This is clearly an important question: it could be that the conflict between the systems is not due to objective differences and incompatibilities, but to problems of management. Given different management the two could well move towards each other or towards some third system under common pressures of technology and human needs. Given management on both sides, that took account of human needs as their priority, instead of élite and role interests, would it matter which, or even what, system prevailed? But given this assumption that the fulfilment of human needs were the goal, all systems would, in due course, adapt correspondingly. Historically, in the movement towards greater participation, greater equality and opportunities for individual development inherent in the movement from slavery, to feudalism, to industrial class relations, to free enterprise, to the welfare state and to socialism, it is in developments of participation, more egalitarianism and a better distribution of resources that there can be hope for the future. The free enterprise systems as they are now being managed, primarily in the interests of established élites, are both a threat to themselves and to world society. On the other hand, under control of centralised élites, the socialist countries are unlikely to develop in ways that ensure their own stability without the same kind of revolutions that brought them into existence in the first place.

In their management both systems require for their continued existence relief from the burden of defence. Both have a common interest in ensuring the internal stability of the other for as long as possible until adjustments can be made. A major contribution would be a significant reduction in arms expenditures. A redefinition of relationships that takes fully into account the internal fears of each, and puts into proper perspective the external threat that each poses for the other, may be a means to this end.

NOTES

1. See pp. 7 and 25.
2. J.M. Keynes, *The General Theory of Employment, Interest and Money* was not, of course, a general economic theory. It was oriented to the particular problems of the day. The last general theory was probably that of Fisher who took a dynamic view of economic development through all its stages.
3. See *Contemporary Economic Problems and Trends.* Horace Taylor, p. 29, 1938 edn.
4. As above.
5. *The Australian Tariff,* by a Committee of Economists set up by the Prime Minister of Australia, the Rt. Hon. S.M. Bruce in 1927, p. 18.
6. *Agricultural Policy, Past Present and Future.* The Empire Economic Union, 1939, p. 10.
7. Taken from the *American Economic Foreign Policy,* by A.D. Gayer and C.T. Schmidt.
8. Compiled from the Australian Census, 1933.
9. As above.

7. Central Government and People

We have argued that élites and authoritative personalities are but symptoms of more basic problems and cannot in themselves be held responsible for failures of management. Even the possibility of their illegal and corrupt behaviour should not be treated as other than the consequences of system properties. Rather than go over the well-explored ground of power élites and personal responsibility of leaders, it is more interesting to ask, 'What can take the place of power élites, or how can they be controlled?' 'Must foreign policy, and major decision-making generally, be left to power élites, to centralised authorities, as though only they have the knowledge and the wisdom that is required?'

There is a dangerous mystique about official decision-making, particularly foreign policy decision-making. The public is persuaded that there is some knowledge resource that is available only to official decision-makers in their capitals, who have 'secret' information. The implication is that this information is the 'truth' and justifies the policies being followed. Outsiders are not in a position to be critical. Where does this information come from? Is diplomatic and intelligence information more reliable than any other kind of information, more reliable than data gathered by overt means and interpreted by persons who have some special knowledge and training in interpretation? Who are the 'experts' who obtain 'secret information', and what is their training? In the USA, is it likely that politically appointed advisers have better 'information' than State Department officials? Is it likely that State Department officials are better informed and have insights that others do not have? When we begin to think about these matters we cannot escape the conclusion that secrecy is little more than a legitimising device, that it is unlikely that officials will have significant knowledge, information and insights about problems of relationships that others do not have. In the 1983 Grenada episode, it soon became clear that those who had taken an interest in the island and the region as a study knew far more than the USA administration, and that the claims of special knowledge were inventions to justify a policy that had domestic political origins.

Secret diplomatic information includes appreciations from foreign posts on local events and policies. They are secret largely because it would be an embarrassment if the information were subject to scrutiny. The secrecy cannot in any sense have the attribution of reliability. In fact, these diplomatic appreciations are frequently culled from each other, from the press, or from sources within foreign governments that may or may not be reliable. There is little deductive reasoning because those concerned are not trained in such a process. They depend almost entirely on empirical data and their prejudices. The unobservable data of motivation and intention cannot be obtained by empirical observations. What is the intention of the Soviet and the USA in arms negotiations? What are the intentions of each when they appear to set out to expand their influence and intervene in the internal affairs of small countries? Attributions of 'aggression', 'world domination' and others are labels that do not have any precise content, and cannot be a basis for policy.

The *Duncan Report* on the British Foreign Office was, unintentionally, a valuable means of demystifying the decision-making processes of the Foreign Office, and of foreign offices generally. The *Report* explicitly stated that, with the exception of lawyers, there was a preference for 'professional generalists'.[1]

This is not to decry the role of governmental institutions. They have their own role in implementing policy. But it is quite absurd to regard people untrained in any discipline at a high level, and wholly untrained in respect to particular areas of behavioural science that are relevant to international relations, as being 'experts' beyond the normal processes of criticism. Furthermore, such officials work within a political framework in which deception and misinformation are tools of the trade.

Nor is this to suggest that scholars would necessarily perform any better in these areas of specialisation. However, they do have two special attributes. First, they can interact more readily without having to maintain positions and in circumstances in which, as scholars, they have a role and a reputation to maintain. In the 1962 inspection debate in Moscow that took place between twenty or so Soviet and US physicists and others, all on both sides began by agreeing with their respective governments. In the course of days each person had to stand up and be counted as a scientist. They agreed very largely on issues over which they had previously been in sharp conflict. In the human relations field, the issues are far more complex, but the same procedures are required so that there is public and scientific scrutiny of policies.

The second attribute is that scholars are accustomed to interacting on a non-disciplinary basis when working together on complex problems. There are few, if any, major problems, including unemployment and defence strategy, that can be resolved within the boundaries of any one or even a few disciplines. The probability is that the knowledge base we require to resolve complex political problems is available, but that what is required is the means by which it can be brought together outside ideological commitment. The process itself extends the knowledge base.

It is for these reasons that there are trends in many countries away from central decision-making by an élite towards more local initiatives. There is an erosion of central authority accompanied, of course, by defensive reactions, including a high level of deception and attempts to curb freedom of information and freedom of the press and popular criticism.

There have been attempts by local governments to declare nuclear free zones. States within the United States have their own foreign trade promotion organisations. People are joining together to protest about the siting of nuclear weapons and even of nuclear energy plants. Is this the beginning of a realisation that central élites, even though elected by 'democratic' processes, do not reflect the common good, and may not be sufficiently expert in specialised fields of policy?

I quote at some length from a talk given in 1982 by Professor Alger of Columbus, Ohio to a gathering in the once devastated city of Yokohama. He adopts a dramatically new approach, one that reflects what is now taking place at a grassroots level, and one that could resolve this serious power élite problem. It will be seen that he has done a lot of soul-searching as a professor of international relations. There are some important implications in what he has to say for the study, teaching and practice of international relations.

You might be curious to know how a professor of international relations came to be so concerned about the international relations of cities. We have traditionally focused our attention on the policies and actions of a few national governmental foreign policy officials, with particular concern for the policies of the big powers. But my personal experiences, as a scholar and citizen over more than a decade, spurred a change of focus. I can briefly summarize this experience for you in the following three points:

First was a growing gap between the world I presented in my teaching and research and that I experienced in my daily life. Gradually I became aware that my personal life was engulfed in international relations that my scholarship and teaching had ignored: the worldwide ties of religious groups, ethnic groups, corporations, youth, women, and a diversity of other human activities. These are not new, but in an age of jet engines and satellite communications they are growing in quantity and importance.

This insight led me to begin to observe more carefully the world around me. Previously my scholarly observations of international affairs had consisted of reading books and documents and talking to people in Washington, at the United Nations in New York and at the specialized agencies of the UN in Geneva, Paris and other cities. But I began observing international relations in the streets, offices and homes of my own city. I became aware of the fact that my professional training had actually been a form of intellectual imprisonment. It had extended my understanding of some international activities—those in foreign offices, summit meetings, the United Nations, NATO, the Warsaw Pact. But this training had prevented me from being able to see the vast sea of international involvements of my daily life and those of other citizens in my city.

This new sense of my personal place in the world led to the *second* reason for my growing interest in the international relations of cities. Like others interested in international affairs, I had long been concerned and puzzled by the fact that the world affairs knowledge of the average citizen in my country is very low. Few people acquire formal education in international affairs. Extensive efforts to improve international education have achieved only limited success, partly because our schools are under local control and there is not widespread local support for more international education. Only gradually did I become aware of the fact that there is a relationship between widespread public ignorance about international affairs and how we have traditionally taught about the world. Because we have tended to teach only about the activities of distant officials—in Washington, Moscow and Tokyo—the subject matter seems distant from the lives of people. What we have traditionally left out of our research and teaching are those things that would link international affairs to the everyday lives of people—the concrete ways in which world systems affect local employment, inflation, environment, migration, etc. This information can make international affairs directly observable and relevant to local people. It shows them how they are connected to things that before seemed distant. Things that had seemed abstract and opaque become concrete and transparent. . . .

The seeds of the *third* reason for my concern with the international relations of cities were sown during the Vietnam War. In my country this was a time of severe trial for people in all walks of life. The war separated people from their national government, divided government itself, and generated conflicts in communities and families throughout the country. Professors of international relations who opposed the war faced a special challenge. Many of the young people taking to the streets, and seizing university buildings, were our students. Why had they, and other citizens, waited so long to voice their opposition to the war? Why were they lashing out in ways that seemed to stiffen the resolve of supporters of the war, thereby polarizing society and intensifying domestic conflict? To what degree had inadequacies in our teaching contributed to citizen ignorance of escalating US involvement in Vietnam and its likely consequences? Why were people largely apathetic for so long before they lashed out in demonstrations and violence? Why did they not act until it was too late to prevent a large scale war—costly in lives, resources and national unity?

Of course, citizen ignorance of what was really going on in Vietnam, beginning in the early 1960s, was not entirely the fault of their teachers. It is customary in all nation-states that citizens do not take part in foreign policy-making—these are matters left to people presumed to have very special insight and competence in the national capital. This is almost as true in the western democracies as in more authoritarian countries. But the Vietnam War vividly revealed, through violence on our streets and university campuses, the potentially cataclysmic consequences of non-participation. When citizens who have not been participating, and who thereby lack knowledge of what is going on, all of a sudden are asked to make great sacrifices, a very dangerous situation is created. Then it is too late for democratic processes to work and people in their frustration lash out at whatever people and institutions are near at hand. This generates a counter-response, in the name of law and order, exemplified in the Vietnam situation by student deaths in Kent State, Ohio, and government surveillance and infiltration of anti-war movements. This kind of polarization could destroy democratic institutions in *any* society.

As a result of personal experiences in these events, and reflections stimulated by these experiences, I was challenged to change my professional agenda. I decided that professors of international relations were contributing to citizen apathy and ignorance about world affairs. I saw how this could lead to the destruction of our democratic institutions. By not helping people to understand how their daily lives are intertwined with world affairs, we have helped to create a false sense of citizen detachment from the world. This false sense of detachment diminishes motivation for learning about world affairs. This contributes to widespread ignorance, supporting the myth that world affairs are too complicated and difficult for most people to understand. The people themselves accept this myth. This destroys even their aspiration to participate. So people leave things to the experts until it is too late to change policies. Then, as in Vietnam, they lash out in frustration.

So I now believe that the foundation stone for world affairs education must be citizen knowledge about the place of their local community in the world. They must know about their ties to distant places through exporting the things they produce, through importing materials for production, through importing things they consume, through participation in transnational, religious and fraternal association, and through world ecological systems that affect the quality of the air they breathe and the quantity and quality of water they consume. . . .

But this would only address one part of the problem— education. There is also the problem of social structure. By this I mean the way in which our society's involvement in the world tends to be controlled from Washington, centralized in ways that even discourages most members of Congress from exerting influence. But there is also a tendency for non-governmental organizations to mirror governmental centralization in foreign affairs. The foreign policies and foreign activities of unions, churches and numerous other voluntary organizations tend to be handled in their national office. Members at large tend not to be consulted. This means that 'recognized' experts in foreign affairs tend to be congregated in a few urban centers. . . .

The concentration of foreign affairs talent in a few central cities deprives the local community of vital resource people that could support local participation in the shaping of foreign policies. Even though experts in world affairs are trained in many cities through- out our country, there are very limited opportunities for these people to practise their profession in these cities. Because the jobs they pursue tend to be concentrated in a few centers, these people are lured to a few urban centers. . . .

But I am concerned that those of us involved in [voluntary] activities are not using our time and resources, toward the end of improving the quality of life on this planet, as effectively as we could. This is because we implicitly tend to accept the social structure for controlling the relations of our society with the world that has been created by custom under the nation-wide system. Although I find many local leaders in international voluntary agencies informed and insightful on world affairs, they still tend to defer to leaders in the national offices of their organizations and even more so to national governmental foreign policy leaders. As a result they tend to acquiesce in a division of labor in which the national office of their organization sets the basic foreign policies for their organization and in which national governmental officials dominate foreign policy choices.

For the most part local people involved in international

activities accept national governmental foreign policies as inevitable, even if they don't agree with them. For example, I believe many internationally active people in Columbus disagree strongly with policies of our present national administration on (1) rising arms expenditures, (2) unwillingness to sign the Law of the Sea Treaty, (3) sending of arms to El Salvador, (4) lack of support for multilateral human rights conventions, and (5) unwillingness to conduct global negotiations with the Third World on a New International Economic Order in the UN. But very few are actively trying to influence governmental policy on these issues. For example, instead of trying to directly affect policy on escalation of arms expenditures and policies on US-Soviet relations, local people involved in international activities tend to have a vague confidence that citizen contacts between US and Soviet citizens will contribute to better US-Soviet relations sometime in the future.

I don't want to be misunderstood. I *do* believe that the more citizen contacts the better, particularly in cases where governments may not be on very friendly terms. But I strongly believe that the prevailing division of labor between local people in voluntary organizations and national officials is preventing local people from doing all they might toward the end of building the kind of world they would like to live in. This division of labor leaves to national governments the task of setting the major lines of foreign policy and leaves to local citizens the task of providing a background of good feeling among networks of citizens. But much of the time citizens are in the predicament of fire brigades, trying to put out, with teacups of water, giant bonfires set by their governments. What I mean is, it is governments that put into motion the main international trends and events, and local citizens are left to deal with the consequences. Arms races create fear and hostility, and citizens are left with the task of trying to overcome this hostility. National and multinational development policies of governments undermine the agricultural sector in the Third World and local citizens are asked to respond with emergency food supplies. Governmments sell arms and wage wars which cause people to flee their homeland. It is then local citizens who are called on to care for the refugees.

But the problem goes even deeper. Because of the division of labor, national governments, in the name of 'national interest', often place limits on the capacity of local citizens to respond to human needs. At times this has prevented US groups from helping people in places like Vietnam and Cuba. Often governments acquire some control over the activities of citizen groups by making money and materials available to them and then placing limits on the use of these materials. This may be by prohibiting distribution to people in countries labelled as 'enemy'. Of course, this tends to undermine the very principles on which most citizen international action is based. Some organizations are quite aware of these problems and fight for their independence, and sometimes even deliberately violate government orders in the name of the values for which they stand. But none the less, the existence of the problems does underline the limits placed on international action by voluntary groups in the context of the division of labor in foreign affairs.

We can now relate this line of argument to our earlier discussion about the importance of local people having knowledge about their place in the world. In my own community I have observed many people who have a humanistic or religiously based impulse to establish contact with and help people throughout the world. This leads to dedicated involvement in 'good works'. They leave basic foreign policy decisions to their national government and usually tend to conduct their 'good works' in ways that do not transgress the 'national interest' reflected in these policies. They even defer to the national office of their voluntary organization with respect to the policies of their organization.

When asked to send food to hungry people, they do so. When asked to find homes and jobs for refugees, they do so. They tend to assume that these 'good works' will have good consequences. So they are not very concerned or even curious about the larger social context of their activities. This prevents them from making personal choices about alternative ways for achieving their objectives. Perhaps instead of settling refugees they should be active against military aid, or military intervention that escalated a local conflict and created a refugee problem. Instead of sending surplus food, perhaps they should be helping people in other countries to grow their own food. But this kind of approach, moving beyond internationalism based on altruistic response to disasters, and potential disasters, requires knowledge about world processes and structures. It also requires a sense of personal responsibility for governmental and non-governmental foreign policies, and competence for making policy decisions—out of their own background and experiences. Instead they tend to defer to élites in distant centers.

If local people are to make their own foreign policy decisions they must perceive their communities as international centers, as places with significant international connections and as places with people quite competent to make decisions about the kinds of connections that would fulfil local needs and values. In my view this must include knowledge about the special place in the world of that local community. Nobody else can speak for the part of this community plays in world systems but the people who inhabit it. By emphasizing local competence and action I certainly do not mean that nations should not have national foreign policies. But what I am saying is that national policies that truly reflect national interests can only come out of a composite of many local interests that flow out of understanding by people in local communities about their place in the world. Present national foreign policies largely reflect the *local* interests of politico-military bureaucracies in the national capital. These interests are imposed on the nation in the cloak of 'national interest'. . . .

Out of this analysis I conclude that cities have a vital role to play in the future of the world. They have a special opportunity, and deep responsibility to educate their inhabitants on the place of their city in the world. This education must begin in kindergarten and extend through university. It must be based on extensive local research and make use of many local examples and resource people. As a result of this kind of education in our cities, people would no longer walk past a bank, factory, or retail shop window without perceiving them as nodes in world systems. In this way people will start to become familiar with complex world systems by learning about them directly through concrete local examples.

As local people learn about world systems near at hand, some will begin to identify issues that are important to them and organize to affect these issues from their local community. Interesting experiments are already underway in many countries to localize action on global issues. Prominent examples that have activated people in my city are (1) Amnesty International through which local groups attempt to free political prisoners in other countries, (2) support of the INFACT boycott against purchase of Nestlé's products because of their marketing practices for baby foods in the Third World, (3) passage of a nuclear freeze resolution by our city council, and (4) vigils and demonstrations at local arms manufacturing plants, such as the North American Rockwell plant in Columbus, Ohio. These developments suggest to me that new potential for local citizen action in world affairs is emerging.

From this I conclude that our cities can become learning communities dedicated to helping citizens to learn how to participate in the whole world. But this will require a collaborative effort of many local activities and organization—schools and universities, adult education organizations, international exchange organizations, foreign aid and relief organizations, refugee organizations, international issue organizations, churches, labor and local government. Each can contribute to international learning—in the classroom, through discussion groups, through participation in exchange programs, through helping people abroad, through helping visitors and new residents from abroad, through becoming active in public policy issues such as disarmament, a new international economic order and human rights. . . .

Efforts to make our cities centers for lifelong learning about the world, and for participating in the world, will lead to growing self-conscious concern about the quality of local relations with the world. I would expect this to stimulate local concern about the degree to which these relations reflect emerging world standards for human relationships on our planet, as revealed in human rights conventions and UN declarations. Only as these emerging standards have meaning for the daily lives of people in their local communities can their promise be fulfilled. . . .

I would expect that these controversies would inevitably draw in people from other cities involved in these relationships. So inter-city dialogue would, through time, lead to inter-city conferences on criteria for evaluating inter-city relations, and perhaps even cooperation in improving the equity of these relationships. Eventually, cities throughout the world might issue declarations, and even draft conventions, that set standards for equitable relations between human settlements. In this way local people would begin to apply widely accepted standards to the inter-city activities of their voluntary associations, business corporations and governments.

As people in cities become more self-conscious participants in the world, it will be important that they avoid the pitfalls of the nation-state system, in which a few big powers dominate the world. A world consisting of equitable relations among human settlements will require both equitable relations between cities, and between cities and smaller settlements—including those in their own countries, as well as those abroad. This approach to the relations of humanity would eventually challenge certain aspects of the nation-state system that we have mentioned earlier. In reality, what is called a nation-state system consists largely of élites in a few primate cities who control world systems largely through controlling access to the world by other cities and towns in their own country.

We are certainly not claiming that the approach we advocate would offer easy solutions to global problems such as poverty, threat of nuclear disaster, human rights and ecological deterioration. But we do believe that this approach would liberate millions of people to join in the pursuit of solutions for these problems. Presently most people are prevented from participating, by their *periphery mentality* and by a *myth of incompetence*. These are a product of their education and socialization. . .

It is very important to make it clear that I am not suggesting that human groupings that transcend cities are not important. In particular, ethnic and nationality groups, with their shared history, language, religion and customs, offer important nurturing environments for people in all parts of the world. People must be free to enjoy and protect the distinctive quality of life to be found in these ethnic and nationality communities. But the more participatory world that I am advocating would offer these communities more possibilities for self-detemination. A great number of ethnic and nationality groups now find it necessary to reply with violence to the violence used by nation-states against their efforts to acquire some degree of autonomy and self-determination.

This talk seems to have focused on the roots of our decision-making problem. Elite monopoly of power and decision-making, operating through bureaucratic organisations at a centre, ensure that policies reflect the interests of structures, institutions, and organised interest groups, but not peoples. Educational systems are designed accordingly. In Britain, in particular, education is arranged so that there is technical education sufficient to keep industry working, and limited opportunities for a general education sufficient only for those who will be part of the adminstrative élite. The US system has the same elements. There is little attempt to educate people generally, to enable them to question assumptions, to reconsider political concepts such as democracy, legitimacy, power, legal norms and others.

It should be noted that this approach is not wholly inconsistent with the US neo-conservative approach to government. It is not inconsistent with the 'get government off people's backs' theme. It is consistent with the approach to education that was adopted in the USA by President Reagan—take the responsiblity for education out of the hands of central government and place it in the hands of local authorities.

The Reagan approach is to conserve funding. Education

needs to be given a high priority in resource distribution if the '1984' syndrome is to be avoided: this is the final defence of human values. Control needs to be local, whether funding is central or local.

The ordinary person has no difficulty in setting down in the broadest terms what he/she seeks: security, justice, identity, recognition, absence of boredom, and others. There is, however, difficulty in translating these personal desires into public policies: the individual is not in a position to determine the public interest or the public policies that would solve or prevent problems occurring.

As a consequence those who assume authority, by one means or another, are in a position to govern on the basis that there are those who have a right to govern and those who have an obligation to obey. After being elected they claim that their policies are legitimised. They arrive at decisions within an ideological thought system that need have no connection with any values or needs of the ordinary person, in whose interests they purport to act.

Now, however, all over the world, there is a situation in which governments have been shown not to understand the complexities of situations any more than the ordinary citizen. Domestic policies have not prevented discontent and violence. International policies have not provided harmonious relations and security.

What would policies look like if they were based on the common person's value systems? What, for example, would be the policy result if the problem of unemployment were tackled on the basis of the highest priority being given to the need for freedom from boredom, for security, for recognition and identity? Would inflation be better or worse? What would be the structural consequences? What interests would suffer in the short and in the long terms? So also with other policies—education, health, defence. Is it clear that the uninformed hunch, the intuitive sense, is a worse basis of policy than the deliberations of élites? An educated society, a society that assumes locally responsibility for policy, is probably the most stable in the longer term.

NOTES

1. See *Report of the Review Committee on Overseas Representation, 1968-9*. Chairman: Sir Val Duncan. Misc. No. 24 (1969).

PART III:

INTERNATIONAL CONSEQUENCES

So far we have been concerned with domestic failures and the political philosophies that have led to these failures. Now we turn to the international scene. In this élite-dominated world society, can smaller states act in ways that prevent the interventions of greater powers? If not, as seems likely for various reasons, is it in the interests of greater powers to avoid competitive involvements in the affairs of smaller states? And if so, how can they do this? Is détente the answer, and where is it inadequate?

This part is the link between a theoretical analysis that is very much concerned with domestic politics and human needs, and the prescriptive notions as applied to the world society that are derived from this theoretical or philosophical approach. It deals, in particular, with the weaknesses of smaller states, and their non-alignment policies, on the one hand, and the dysfunctional policies of intervention of the great powers, on the other. It anticipates some alternative strategies that are in the interests of both.

8. The Failure of the United Nations

We have argued that conflict in the international society is to a large degree, if not almost entirely, a spillover of domestic conflict. We have rejected the 'billiard ball model' of world society as being quite unrealistic: relations between states are not just between their outer surfaces. Yet the United Nations Charter specifically excludes jurisdiction over matters that are domestic.[1] This prevents the United Nations becoming involved in domestic conflicts, unless it can be shown that they are a matter of international concern. For example, no intervention is possible in the affairs of South Africa that keep spilling over to other African states; conflicts in Northern Ireland and many other countries are outside its scope. The conventional wisdom and political theory when the Charter was drafted, now some 40 years ago, were false.

From a practical point of view, it was probably wise to exclude domestic conflicts from the purview of the United Nations. If factions within states were free to refer disputes to the world body it would be overwhelmed, since most states have dissatisfied minorities and majorities, of which only some are crucial in the world society, and most are better dealt with by domestic processes.

And here lies the problem. Many conflicts that are domestic in origin spill over into the international system.

Great powers and larger states intervene, sometimes by invitation, sometimes on their own initiative. They can take advantage of a domestic conflict to destabilise further the local situation for their own strategic advantage. And the United Nations has no jurisdiction. But the domestic processes for resolving conflict are frequently those of coercion and violence that invite external intervention. In practice, the world system has no means of handling conflicts for it has no processes whereby sources of conflict can be dealt with.

In this perspective it is irrelevant to complain about the use of the veto in the Security Council, since without it the world body is powerless to intervene in the type of conflict that is the source of international conflict.

It could reasonably be argued that there is no solution to the problem, short of revolution within all states that have unstable political systems, that there cannot be peace until there is stability within every member state of the world society. Indeed, both superpowers claim that peace will only be secured when the world society comprises states pursuing their particular type of political system. Neither side is prepared, apparently, to allow states to evolve according to their own requirements and towards forms that may be inconsistent with the political philosophies of the contending powers. In these circumstances, a homogeneous world could result only from the world domination of one great power or the other, presumably after nuclear war. It was this problem to which détente addressed itself. Later we shall examine this approach which is, of course, outside the framework of the United Nations and a recognition of its irrelevance in its present form.

A second source of the United Nations' failure is in its peace settlement processes. The conventional wisdom in 1945 was simply that there were certain norms to be observed within a society and that observance of these was to be enforced, if necessary, by central authorities. Settlement processes were, therefore, by judicial processes or by arbitration. Where norms seemed not to be applicable, the processes were bargaining and negotiation. The Charter, as a consequence, was concerned with peaceful 'settlement': the idea that conflicts needed to be 'resolved'—in other words that they presented problems to be solved—was not within conventional wisdom.

Indeed, it was not until the early 1960s that this notion was first entertained, and then it was in the field of industrial relations.[2] Even then it was difficult for international lawyers to come to terms with the irrelevance of traditional settlement processes. A group of lawyers writing at about the same time argued that the processes of judicial settlement, arbitration, mediation and negotiation were adequate. All that was wrong was that the parties to disputes were unwilling to resort to them.[3] Theory and experience lead us to believe that representatives of parties to disputes, be they governments or industrial leaders, will not allow decision-making to be taken out of their hands and placed in the hands of courts or arbitrators. It is their role to preserve and to determine values and interests. They cannot afford to have decisions forced on them on important matters of values. Decision-making must be open up to the point of final decision, in which they must be involved directly.

However, the criticism is not fundamentally a criticism of the United Nations as a world organisation, but of the political thinking that was behind the drafting of the Charter and which persists today. If there were the necessary changes in political thought, the interpretation of the Charter would also change. For example, if it were now the consensus view that domestic influences and failings are the source of international conflict, then many matters now regarded as a matter of domestic jurisdiction would be treated as a matter of international concern, and brought within the purview of the United Nations, regardless of the claims of the parties concerned.

This, however, would not solve the problem. The second criticism refers to means of dealing with conflicts. Forcing solutions on parties is no means of resolving a conflict and, in practice, is rarely possible. The issue is not whether a matter is within the jurisdiction of the United Nations, but whether there are techniques and processes which parties to disputes willingly seek out as a means of avoiding its costs and consequences. These must be problem-solving processes that achieve win-win outcomes, and not outcomes that happen to accord with some set of international norms that are unacceptable to the parties. United Nations adversary debates, bargaining and power negotiation are not relevant to sensitive issues of security, identity and recognition of nations, ethnic groups and communities with special cultural values.

These two failings are the same dominant failings of the political systems that are represented at the United Nations. Just as it is not possible for a domestic political system to be stable if élite norms are being forced on members, so it is in the international system. The norms of diplomacy are great power norms that allow espionage, and other misuses of diplomatic immunities, that are of little advantage to smaller states. The norms of trade and finance are the norms of those states that have trading and financial advantages. When majorities at the United Nations or its agencies demonstrate against the application of such norms, then the United Nations appears to the greater powers as being dysfunctional, and support is threatened. Thus it is that the problem comes back to problems of political structures and the political philosophies that underpin these structures. Underlying this problem is the problem of change where élite values and interests are threatened. Underlying this problem is the problem of process by which such conflicts of interest can be resolved in ways that take into account the costs and consequences of resistance to change and that explore options that meet the needs of those concerned.

It follows that the United Nations Secretary General and his staff have an impossible job. They are bound by certain approaches and processes that cannot succeed. Inevitably, they must become either defensive or critical of the whole process—as indeed has been the Secretary General in his 1982 Report to the General Assembly.[4] But it is not for them to set a new direction, it is for member states—or perhaps the agencies and organs of the United Nations, such as the United Nations University—to endeavour to bring the United Nations into line with contemporary situations and knowledge.

NOTES

1. Chapter 1, 'Purposes and Principles', Article 2 para. 7 of the United Nations Charter contains this 'domestic jurisdiction' clause.

2. See Blake, Shepard and Moulton's *Managing Intergroup Conflict in Indistry*. This was published in 1964. While its message will not seem unusual now, it was then innovative, such has been the shift in thinking and in the practice of industrial relations.

3. The David Davies report was written by a group of international lawyers who held that existing institutions were adequate, all that was lacking was a will to use them. Since this time it has become clear that the institutions were not used because they took decision-making out of the direct control of parties to disputes.

4. The Report of the Secretary General, Javier Perez de Cuellar, 1982.

9. The Zonal-Functional System

Throughout the preceding chapters we have argued that traditional notions of central politics have imposed limits on western thinking about both domestic and international problems. The beliefs that central authorities have a right and duty to impose law and order in accord with their norms, that they should have a legitimized monopoly of force for this purpose and that societies should be 'integrated', are deeply ingrained in the thinking of western governing authorities. It is also a fundamental tenet of all single-party or authoritarian systems. We have argued in the previous chapter that the United Nations has powers so restrictive that it is not in a position to deal with many conflicts that are defined as domestic, yet have far-reaching international implications.

It is useful to pause at this stage and examine an option that is open to states experiencing the kind of ethnic conflict that spills over so readily into the international society.

Many societies throughout the world are facing the complicated domestic problem of how to deal constitutionally with a multi-ethnic or culturally-divided society in ways which reduce power confrontations among the divisions, that preserve the values each holds to be important and that, also, reduce the dangers of external interference.

The problem is an old one. However, it has become more

widespread and acute in recent decades for a variety of reasons. Independence, after a long period of colonialism, led to the removal of a controlling third party, thus inviting power confrontations among factions that had not been integrated into one community. Since independence there has been a greater awareness of the rights of minorities, and a greater reluctance to accept 'rights' accorded in a paternalistic way, or by reason of a constitutional requirement, to minorities by majorities. There is a greater physical ability of the minorities to assert their claims, frequently assisted by interested foreign powers. There is a world system in which great powers have a strategic interest in supporting factions within states. There is increased communications among the same ethnic and cultural groups in different countries, leading to mutual encouragement and assistance.

Countries facing problems of ethnicity at present include Northern Ireland, Cyprus, Zimbabwe, South Africa, Sri Lanka, Lebanon, Malaysia, Fiji, Israel—perhaps most nations in which ethnicity has become an important political factor, including the Soviet Union. The majority of nations in Europe, Africa, the Middle East and Asia are experiencing the problem in one form or another whether at an early or advanced stage. Each considers its own problems as unique. The solutions required probably are unique in the sense that certain local conditions must be met. On the other hand, they have many features in common, and must, in all cases, deal with these common features. They relate to values that are universal: in every national group there is value attached to language, to religion and to culture generally. There is value attached to symbols of identification and to opportunities to demonstrate this identification with the community, sometimes extending to physical separateness, even the right to discriminate in employment and association. There is value attached to the security of the ethnic group as an entity, despite its smallness of number. Most important of all, and most difficult to provide for politically, there is value attached to independent decision-making in areas affecting values, without the compromises and paternalistic 'rights' accorded within a power-sharing political system.

Failure to meet these fundamental needs leads, inevitably,

to community organisation, political pressures and, finally, when these do not achieve the required results, to violence in one form or another. This is a situation of dedication to a cause that encourages terrorism. It also leads to external interventions if greater powers perceive some strategic gain.

It may reasonably be asked why such long-standing and serious problems have not been tackled with more vigour and success. The explanation appears to be that it has been within western tradition that societies should be integrated by a socialisation process that promotes shared values, backed by sanctions imposed by central authorities. The western concept of majority rule mitigates against ethnic identity and security, while at the same time failing in practice to achieve equality of treatment, non-discrimination and equal recognition of different cultural values. Modifications to majority rule, such as power-sharing and constitutional rights accorded to the minority by the majority, have failed in practice to satisfy the needs of ethnic identity. Western political philosophy cannot cope with conceptual notions that give a positive connotation to separateness, human needs that defy the socialisation process, challenges to the right of central authorities to impose what they argue to be consensual values, and to demands for the pursuit of community interests that, to the central authorities, may seem to be incompatible with their perception of state interests. Marxism, which is a part of western political philosophy, endeavours to overcome the problem by arguing that ethinicity is merely a special case of class: some anthropologists cannot accept this.[1]

This is a problem that can be solved only by a fundamental paradigm shift in which the human needs of individuals and of groups are incorporated into constitutional structures instead of being subject to the requirements of political structures. Indeed, this is a shift that is required even in mono-ethnic societies in which feudal institutions deny to their members the basic human needs of identity and participation, leading to the same kinds of resistance and organised violence.

The contemporary ethnicity problem had its origins in great power expansion and colonialism. National boundaries were established that cut across tribal and ethnic groups and which incorporated such groups within one state. Further tensions were created under colonial rule when one faction, frequently a minority whose security depended on the good-will of the colonial power, was selected as the law-enforcing faction. Particular factions were left to carry on after colonial rule and sometimes given a dominant position by the independence constitution, as was the case with Malaysia. Once independence had led to the withdrawal of the controlling external power, power confrontations were possible among the different groups that had not been integrated into one social community. In recent years, throughout the world, there has been a greater awareness of the rights of minorities, a greater reluctance to accept 'rights' paternalistically accorded under a majority rule constitution, and a greater ability of minorities to assert their claims by violence and sometimes through the help of external powers.

The problem has been accentuated and situations of violence have been created by responses that are logically dictated by western political philosophy. Defining situations as minority rebellion against majority rule, and trying to impose some integrated structure such as a federation, has created more problems than solutions. Federations are a result of integrative behaviour, as in Australia and other stable federations. If multi-ethnic societies are to become integrated, then it has to be through the long process of integrative behaviour that is stimulated by the security and identity made possible by separateness.

There are many reasons why this should be so. In every case there are leaders of factions each seeking an authoritative role. Unity discussions usually centre on role allocations and frequently break down for this reason. There are arguments about power-sharing that cannot be resolved within a bargaining framework. The numbers game does not establish a just society: minorities can never accept a second-class citizen status. Breakdown in talks inevitably leads to higher levels of inter-communal tension. These are all the higher because the factions concerned are close physically and frequently share national norms which each accuses the other of infringing. As in families, emotional involvements lead to higher, not lower, levels of violence when conflict occurs.

The conclusion seems to be that what already exists must form the basis of any new structure. In Cyprus there were communal Chambers. The state became divided ethnically even more as a result of conflict and of external interventions. Any new structure has to be built on the existing realities of separate communities. Any attempt to impose some preconceived constitutional structure because it has worked elsewhere, or because it accords with certain legal norms, is bound to fail. So, too, in Northern Ireland. The preconceived notion of 'democracy' or rule by the majority with certain modifications to provide some token participation must fail. While educated middle-class élites and professional people who travel widely can bridge this ethnic gap, for the great majority of people there is a strong desire to live in communities, preserve cultures and achieve security through identity with what is familiar, while at peace with, and with tolerance of, the wider society.

There is an obvious dilemma. On the one hand, there is a reluctance on the part of the communities concerned and of the world society to accept separation of communities and the creation of small non-viable states. On the other, integration of different ethnic and cultural communities seems not to be possible by agreement. What is the answer to this dilemma?

It would appear that some means needs to be found to give communities the security that independence and separateness provide. Movements towards greater inter-dependence and even integration can come only by the mobility that develops out of this security, whereas a forced dependence or integration creates insecurities.

Territory has always been an important source of identification and security. A zonal system is one that makes this possible for each community. Each has an area administered solely by the community. Any member who opts to live outside that area does so on the clear under-standing that he/she becomes subject to the rules and conventions that pertain in the area into which he/she moves. The right of movement, subject to this requirement, is, however, unlimited: the whole state is one in the sense that there is an identification with the state as well as with the group or nation.

Matters that are of common concern are negotiated on a functional basis; that is, by officials who act as specialists in respect of particular administrative areas. Just as there are in the international society functional agreements concerning health, post and communications, and civil aviation, so in relations between communities. The agreements are negotiated subject to ratification by each community's authorities. In this sense each has a veto. It is a veto that is exercised with caution, and only when some community interest is involved for fear of threatening a greater value, that is, the value attached to the integrity of the total society.

In this way the political process is confined to local and cultural matters that are of more immediate political concern, leaving all other matters to specialists who operate subject to political sanctions.

In traditional political institutions, where relative power and bargaining processes determine decisions, agreement among community leaders is difficult on most matters. Leaders feel they must take public stances. For example, if the decision were in relation to representation at the United Nations, the majority faction would feel obliged to claim the right. In a non-bargaining framework many other options are available: rotation, selection on the basis of individual experience and qualifications, joint missions, and others. Functional arrangements of this kind are usually more efficient and professional than those made in public debate by political representatives operating in an adversary structure.

The zonal-functional approach seems to be the realistic one to multi-ethnic organisations. It provides a physical area with which there can be cultural and ethnic identification, without limiting the opportunity to live within and identify with a wider state society. It provides political leadership and leadership roles in respect of matters that are politically important, that is, matters that deal with the lives of peoples within communities. The fact of separateness eliminates sources of tension and of power rivalries. This, in turn, reduces the possibilities of external interference and external support to one faction or another in a power rivalry. Matters that are in common are dealt with, as they need to be in complex modern societies whose domestic policies affect the international system, as technical matters for specialists to handle outside party politics, yet with a political sanction in the background. At the same time mobility between communities is possible, which would tend to increase as interactions increase, leading to some degree of effective integration.

There is one procedural aspect that deserves mention. The conceptual notion of a zonal system requires adaptation to each separate situation and innovations relevant to it. It is most unlikely that representatives of communities, previously or currently in conflict, can sit down together and evolve a zonal system that meets their needs. If bargaining and power confrontations are to be avoided, then the specialist or functional approach needs to be pursued from the outset. This probably requires an exploratory discussion under the control of a panel of facilitators who can ensure a problem-solving approach and the avoidance of power- and role-bargaining. The values of the communities that finally have to be catered for do not come into focus when leadership power and role are the main concern. Whether it be at arms control negotiations at the international level, or considerations of constitutional devices at the inter-communal level, there is an important and even indispensable role for the professional facilitator whose job it is, not to make proposals and suggestions, but to assist those concerned in analysing in depth the values they seek to pursue and the motivations and intentions of each other.

It may well be that there are other ways of dealing with typical communal problems within the one state. What is clear is that attempts to arrive at solutions within our traditional political approaches are unlikely to succeed. When the British Foreign Secretary, Lord Carrington, met the parties from Rhodesia at Lancaster House, London, he presented them with a draft independence constitution, drawn up to provide a central authority and an integrated state. The tribal problem was thus glossed over. It was this that should have been discussed first so that the draft constitution to be negotiated would contain within it a resolution of the problem of different communities within the one state. The starting-point of any successful constitutional innovation is a consideration of the values of the communities and how they can be met. It is the parties that can show inventiveness by making clear their minimal demands. It is for political theorists or facilitators to ensure that they are met and that ethnic communities are not expected to conform to preconceived and unacceptable constitutional devices. Proposals that come from mediators, especially mediators who reflect great power strategic interests, are unlikely to meet either the needs of the communities or the longer-term strategic interests of the great powers.

NOTES

1. This argument has been developed by Enloe, p.268.

10. The Role of Smaller States

If a major problem in the relations of the great powers is instability in smaller states, the question arises whether smaller states could help to reduce great power confrontations by themselves resisting interventions. If this is not possible, then the full responsibility for avoiding confrontations over conflicts within smaller states is forced back on to the great powers. We shall deal with this in the next chapter.

Before there can be norms of intervention that will effectively isolate the great powers struggle from the rest of the world society, two conditions are necessary. First, a realisation by the great powers that avoidance of competitive interventions is in their strategic and survival interests. Second, a realisation by small states that it is their interests to be genuinely independent, non-aligned and in full control of their own affairs. The former is a politically realistic possibility, provided there were means available, for it is more and more apparent that great power confrontation is likely over third states and the preservation of spheres of influence. The latter is less likely, but the smaller states concerned have often invited such interventions.

In the immediate post-war period, under the leaderships of Nehru in India, and Nasser in Egypt, there was a prospect that independence and neutrality, rather than alliance, could be the norm in international relations. The non-aligned movement was beginning to create a new type of international society that could have isolated great power conflict.[1]

However, the non-aligned movement has failed in its objectives. The reasons are not hard to find. There are not many small states that can claim a legitimised status. Many, if not most, are under threat internally. Sometimes the reasons are environmental and structural: boundaries that were drawn up by colonial powers cut across ethnic groups and incorporated factions that make a unified state impossible. Sometimes the regimes are a carry-over from the colonial past and are governed by small privileged groups that have learned western philosophies and who try to insist on their rights to rule, by coercion and repression if necessary. Whatever the reasons, there are not many newly-created states that can survive without foreign military assistance. Most seek to be part of an alliance or to receive assistance in dealing with internal opposition. There cannot be non-alignment in conditions of internal instability that requires alliance support.

This élite and non-legitimised rule has characteristic features. It is popular to attribute many of the problems of underdeveloped countries to the activities of multinational corporations. This is scapegoating. International corporations can be controlled by state authorities that are prepared to act in the interests of development and not take advantage of corporations to pursue their own interests. Not only is bribery widespread in dealings with the activities of large international enterprises, which is clearly something within the control of governments; more serious is the fact that the factories corporations create and the goods that they produce are frequently wholly unsuited to the needs of the developing countries concerned. Luxury goods of all kinds are consumed by a small élite, whereas it is agricultural equipment and simple means of transport that are required. In short, the existence of gross inequalities of income in the developing states leads to distortions in the economy that prevent development. This is not the fault of corporations: it is the direct consequence of the behaviour of governing élites.

Corruption and the pursuit of élite interests in developing countries is but a symptom of a far greater problem that underlies the great powers conflict. If there were any move in any developing country towards a more egalitarian system, in which agriculture were promoted and the drift to cities were thereby discouraged, there would be anxiety in the West. Such a movement would be interpreted as socialist. Those in whose interest it was to resist such trends would appeal for western help. This raises the wider issue of problems of change, to which we turn later. The point is made here only that in given post-colonial circumstances, and in the present international environment, it is not to be expected that small states will make any contribution to the improvement of East-West relations by discouraging great power interventions in their affairs.

There are smaller and middle powers that are in a position to act with more independence towards the great powers and to place limits on their opportunities for confrontation. They include states such as India, Australia, Japan, some Western and perhaps Eastern European states and many others which value their independence, yet have accepted major incursions into their free decision-making processes and even their constitutional processes. To date they have been cowed by the great powers and seem to have attributed to them a monopoly of wisdom. How absurd it is for the Soviet Union and the United States to be engaged in arms control talks affecting Europe without European powers being present! Many have foreign bases on their soil and, on some occasions, through their own inaction, have had political change forced on them when there was a suspicion that these bases were to be brought under some control or eliminated. However, change seems to be on the way. There is less and less confidence in great power decision-making and more and more resistance to decisions being made without consultation. While it is easy to quote cases in the West, such as missile deployment and the American invasion of Grenada and unilateral decisions in the Middle East, it can be assumed that Eastern European states are reacting the same way.[3]

A London group of scholars have recently published a book in which they advocate for Britain a policy of 'concerned independence'.[4] They are not suggesting neutrality, non-alignment or isolation. On the contrary, they are suggesting an active policy of intervention in East-West relations, almost a modern version of the power-balancing role that Britain is thought once to have played. The emphasis is on 'concern'—that is, direct interventions to facilitate improved relations between the great powers. A higher level of independence would be an important part of this. A movement among such middle powers in Europe, Asia and Latin America is probably the only means by which the great powers will finally be constrained in their confrontations.

There are areas in which such smaller states could make significant contributions and in so doing regain some of their lost independence. Smaller states that are secure internally have no wish to intervene in the affairs of others, except to the extent that they might be asked to do so by a government that has strong democratic support and seeks some kind of technical or other assistance for its legitimate development. They are not interested in giving assistance to governments to compensate for lack of internal support. For this reason they tend to believe in open diplomacy. They have no desire to establish within the capital of another state a walled citadel or foreign enclave in which and from which any activity, legal or illegal, can be perpetuated. They have, therefore, no need for diplomatic immunity as traditionally interpreted.

Diplomatic immunity is an important international issue. It is on record that crimes from theft to murder have been committed without waiver of diplomatic immunity. Even such crimes are dwarfed in significance by other diplomatic abuses. Interventions in the domestic affairs of nations by greater powers, espionage and counter-espionage activities, the promotion of political instability, even the removal of governments from office in 'friendly states' are not unknown.

Diplomatic immunity was the creation of great powers intent upon extending their influence and protecting their spheres of interest against political and social change. Diplomacy itself was a creation in times in which there were no quick means of communication between governments. Diplomacy itself is in question in an age of instant communication. However the immunity that goes with diplomacy is not merely irrelevant in a global system of independent states, but is a source of tension and conflict among small and large states alike. Immunity is not important to small states, especially ones that have nothing to hide, that believe in open diplomacy and do not operate in a power framework of intrigue and misinformation. Far from assisting the management of world society in its quest for peace and security, diplomatic immunity is a destabilising influence.

It is open to smaller states to renegotiate their diplomatic agreements and to bring up to date an outmoded system and, in so doing, preserve their independence and freedom from unacceptable foreign interference. This could be of great benefit to the great powers in helping them disengage. However, it does seem that the smaller the state the more its politicians and diplomats value the privileges of diplomatic immunity. They would probably be unwilling to make such sacrifices, just as they are unwilling to curb the activities of multinational corporations.

There are many ways in which smaller and middle powers could work together to help the great powers to disengage. However, they are all so caught up in the Left-Right, East-West, communist-capitalist divide that positive approaches seem not to be likely for domestic reasons, at least without clear and agreed signals from the great powers.

For these reasons we have to conclude that responsibility is forced back on the great powers for the control of their own behaviour. The smaller states have a role to play; but only if the great powers see it to be in their interests for them to play such a role. This presupposes that the great powers both wish to avoid a test of strength and to find some non-violent means of resolving their ideological conflict.

NOTES

1. See Burton, *International Relations: A general theory* (1965), in which it was argued that non-alignment was the 'norm' of international behaviour rather than alliance relationships.
2. Goulet has argued that, for such reasons, the term 'liberation' is to be preferred to 'development'. There are prior domestic conditions that have to be met before there can be freedom from foreign interference in development.
3. After the Soviet walk out of arms control negotiations in November 1983, a statement was made by Romanian Communist Party officials saying that the USA and the USSR should resume discussions. On 16 November the President, Nicolae Ceausescu, called on both countries to renounce the deployment of new missiles.
4. This is a book by Burton *et al* that argues that the role of middle powers such as Great Britain should be to stand between the great powers, not as a neutral or in isolation, but in order to play a positive third-party role.

11. Soviet-American Relations: Legal Norms

On both sides of the great divide there is a high level of missionary zeal expressed. Both ideologies provide a basis for claiming a special mission and malign the intentions of those who espouse the other. Consequently, the idea of competition suggests itself: 'coexistence'. Provided this could be peaceful competition there would be no great strategic concern. However, when what is at stake is a system and its survival, competition cannot be peaceful.

In 1974 the Soviet international lawyer, Tunkin, argued that Soviet foreign policy rested on the fundamental principles of international law. There exist many international treaties among socialist states that provide for requests for assistance, and for obligations to render assistance of all kinds. Soviet foreign relations are based on these.

The political justification for the making of such treaties and for the creation of a 'socialist internationalism' was, in Tunkin's words, 'The experience of the world socialist system has confirmed the necessity for the closest union of those countries breaking away from capitalism.'[1]

The same legal case, based on agreements entered into, can be made by those whose ideological commitment is to capitalism. Furthermore, western policies are based on essentially the same political arguments that Tunkin put forward to justify Soviet policies of assistance to smaller states. We need to remind ourselves that this is not a one-sided position: there is the same urge to dominate.

The missionary power orientation is so strong in the United States, carrying with it the belief that it is only the Soviet Union that is the 'aggressor', that it is important to place discussion of norms in the setting of American performance. The following is a short article by George Ball, published in The New York Times, 14 —June 1983. (George Ball was Under-Secretary of State in the Kennedy and Johnson administrations.)

Under the so-called Brezhnev Doctrine, Moscow claims the right to intervene in its sphere of influence, Eastern Europe, whenever 'internal and external forces hostile to socialism' try 'to turn the development' of a socialist country 'towards the restoration of a capitalist regime'. In what is historically considered our sphere, we pursue a reverse Brezhnev Doctrine, intervening in Latin America whenever we find a capitalist country is threatened with a socialist regime. We do not do it very well.

Our doctrine was first enunciated in 1928 when Calvin Coolidge sent our marines back to Nicaragua—acting, he said, to save it from 'Bolshevism' imported from Mexico, which served then as our Communist bogeyman. When we withdrew eight years later, we rewarded the Nicaraguans with the dynastic Somoza dictatorship, which, for the next 43 years, tyrranized the people and stole everything in sight.

In 1954, Dwight D. Eisenhower authorized the Central Intelligence Agency to 'destabilize' the legitimately elected Guatemalen Government of President Jacobo Arbenz, who had shown the bad judgement to accept the political support of a small Communist Party and arms from Czechoslovakia and—even more heinous—had expropriated United Fruit company properties. Our country's bequest to the Guatemalan people was a succession of brutal right-wing military regimes punctuated by assassinations.

In 1961, the Kennedy Administration confirmed our reverse Brezhnev Doctrine by launching the Bay of Pigs, which, by its ignominious failure, strengthened rather than dislodged Fidel Castro's hold on Cuba.

In 1965, Lyndon B. Johnson sent 400 marines to the Dominican Republic to rescue Americans reported under fire; then, when J.

Edgar Hoover discovered 53 known Communists there, he followed that deployment with 22,000 troops. That this time the story had a happy ending was only because a superb diplomat, Ellsworth Bunker, spent a year in the tawdry rooms of a rundown hotel in the Dominican capital. By excruciating patience, he achieved what the Reagan Administration has refused even to undertake in El Salvador—an arranged settlement between the contending parties.

In 1973, the Nixon Administration undertook to 'destabilise' the legitimately elected Chilean Government of President Salvador Allende, but before it could make its clumsy efforts effective, the inept regime destabilised itself. Chile was rewarded with the regime of Gen. Augusto Pinochet—one of the more bloody-minded tyrants in modern Latin American history.*

If the world system of states were unambiguously separated into systems of socialist and of capitalist states, if, that is, each of the great powers had mutually agreed spheres of influence which embraced the whole globe, the Tunkin norms of international law could be applied: two separate political systems would exist in peaceful coexistence. Their interactions, commercial and other, would be within a framework of norms established by the two great powers. Internal change in smaller states that altered the political system would not be allowed to take place. Each great power would respect the sovereign integrity of the other and the rights of each to dominate its sphere of influence. There could be mutual cooperation on environmental matters of common concern and some measure of interdependence in relationships.

The pre-1939 world system, in which almost all small nations were incorporated into a few colonial systems, had some of the features of this model. Each recognised the sphere of influence of the others, and internal change within a colonial country was unlikely.

This model, however, does not accord with the essential features of the contemporary world society. There are not just two sets of states, socialist and capitalist, however much the great powers would like to have it this way. There are many states that cannot so readily be classified. There is a third set that overlaps the two, the units within it having some features of the one and some of the other. There are qualitative differences that prevent states being placed in either an international socialist or an international capitalist system. Furthermore, unlike the colonial era, in contemporary times members of the mixed set are often in a position to resist foreign intervention and control. Even though structurally in one set or the other, states are sometimes able to align themselves with the other set in international institutions and to vote or act against their set's leadership. Indeed, even members of the two main sets are at times resistant to external controls in their domestic affairs. This is the experience within the socialist international system no less than in the capitalist sphere of influence. The drive towards separate identity and separate political development will become more, and not less, intense with time: communications, values attached to certain human needs, technology and resource development and many other influences will further weaken metropolitan control over spheres of influence.

Tunkin presents an ideal-type model. Intellectually, it resolves the conflict between power and norms of international socialism by depicting the world society as socialist-capitalist. In so doing it defines away the problems of confrontation over mixed systems that are the cause of conflict. The model would be nearer reality and focus on the essential problems if it included a principle or norm that is implied logically, but excluded in Tunkin's exposition. This is the principle or norm that, in the pursuit of international socialism (or international capitalism) the same 'principle of comradely mutual assistance' applies to factions within states, giving them the right 'to obtain assistance from other socialist [capitalist] states'. This is observed by both East and West in practice, if not in theory and exposition. This principle was the justification for Soviet intervention in Afghanistan and for the United States intervention in Vietnam. Both would argue, of course, that their interventions were made necessary by the prior intervention of the other. Under this principle, any minority, be it in authority or in rebellion, can exercise the right to seek assistance. Because of the nature of underdevelopment and past imperial authorities, Soviet intervention is usually in support of a minority in rebellion and trying to change the system. For the same reasons, United States intervention is usually in support of authorities under threat. But whichever it is, the principle is the same: there is a right of intervention whenever it is sought. This means, in practice, whenever either competing great power believes that it can gain influence or retain influence.

The application of this principle raises all manner of difficult issues of legitimacy: should it be assumed that 'recognised' or legal authorities have a right to expect external support despite lack of internal electoral support? Should it be assumed that the internal processes of revolt and rebellion automatically attract external assistance on some grounds of justice? These issues are at the core of the problem of competitive intervention.

In practice, there are no differences between Soviet and United States policies in this respect: both intervene on the side of favoured factions. There are differences in moral justifications and political rhetoric; but the processes are the same. There is, however, an important difference in the deductive conclusions arrived at by each side. On the Soviet side it is claimed that 'peaceful coexistence' and 'detente' are possible in East-West relations, whereas the United States adopts the view that in the present circumstances only confrontations are possible. The latter appears to be the more logical position. Within nations within each set and in the third mixed set, there are continuous struggles for change and for élite power. There is, therefore, competition and conflict between the great powers to maintain or to expand their sphere of influence by assistance to conducive governments and factions. These are not conditions in which there can be peaceful coexistence or détènte. The principles and norms logically implied in the Tunkin analysis, and followed by both sides, necessarily lead to conflict between the great powers.

This could be put another way: the notion of domestic jurisdiction is an irrelevant one. International conflict does not exist as a separate phenomenon. International conflict is a spillover of domestic conflict. The principles and norms of international law are inadequate unless they recognise that international relations is an abstract: we are concerned with a world society in which national boundaries have little practical relevance. Peaceful coexistence between competing ideologies is not possible in conditions in which other states are in a process of political change.

In this sense Tunkin did not resolve the conflict, even in theory, between the observance of legal norms and the use of power. Both sides in the contemporary struggle pursue their missionary goal of conversion and give support to the converted. They do this for power reasons no doubt; but no less they do this out of a sense of commitment and dedication to a cause. Both believe the other to be infringing norms when there is any such intervention. Both can, at the same time, justify their own intervention in the affairs of others as defence against the subversive influences of the other. Both confront each other in disputed regions with all the power at their disposal. Both are self-righteous. Both believe the other treacherous and not to be believed. Both become devious and employ practices outside diplomatic norms. Both expend resources on defence and feel threatened by the defence strategies of the other. From their respective positions, both are in the right and expect the support of their own peoples, of their allies, and of world opinion.

It is this mirror image that underlies the failure of arms negotiations, tensions over interventions, abuse of diplomatic immunity, fears of subversion and the many other problems of East-West relations. The Soviet view is clearly valid: there has to be peaceful coexistence between the two different systems if there is not to be war. But how? In this framework détente can only mean tolerance of behaviour by both sides that is ultimately unacceptable to the United States. As a continuous process détente can only mean the opportunity for peaceful subversion by the Soviet Union. It can only mean that socialism has some kind of priority over other forms of government and should be allowed to proceed without opposing influences. In this framework, freedom, as defined by the United States, can only mean tolerance of behaviour by both sides that is ultimatley unacceptable to the Soviet Union. As a continuous process, freedom, as defined can only mean the opportunity of peaceful subversion by the United States. It can only mean that capitalism and the free enterprise system have some kind of priority over other forms of government and should be allowed to proceed without opposing influences.

It is clear that there is somewhere in this power-normative reasoning a logical flaw; an element is missing in this essentially ideological orientation. The declared goals are the same: peace, prosperity and freedom (even though each of these may be defined differently according to ideology and culture). There are conflicts in tactics rather than goals. If this were the case, it could be assumed that both sides would accept the need for change in the promotion of welfare and justice, especially change in the sphere of influence of the other, but also in many cases in countries in their own sphere. Both sides, none the less, resist change promoted by the other. Has the essence of the problem they face something to do with the process of change, resistance to change by indigenous élites, and the absence of agreed means by which change can be promoted and resistance by powerful majority or minority élites overcome? Is the source of tension and potential conflict the aim by one or both rivals to pursue world domination of its system, or is it a nervousness about change, which both perceive to be necessary and inevitable, and about its unknown character and consequences? Is this why the West bolsters repressive regimes, and why the Soviet seeks to prevent liberal moves in Poland and elsewhere?

There are two distinct issues here. There is the issue of change and change processes: how can change be brought about smoothly, without violence, without inviting interventions and by means that achieve sought purposes? There is a second issue that cannot be ignored: that the intentions of one or both great powers are, indeed, world domination for its own sake: the malign-benign issue.

Both of these require attention before we can move to consider prescription. Both relate to the definition of Soviet-USA relationships out of which prescription emerges. We shall deal with the malign-benign issue first.

NOTES

1. See Tunkin, p. 435.

12. The Hidden Data: Motivations and Intentions

Attributing the Soviet-United States confrontation in world society to problems of change reflects a benign definition of the problem. There may well be sinister motivations for control and power for its own sake, or through some ideological commitment. The aim could well be the final elimination of all opposing systems, rather than any longer-term evolution of altered systems under the pressures of technological change and human demands.

Certainly, the President of the United States assumed this to be the case in 1983. On the occasion of his visit to Tokyo he was quoted as referring to 'an adversary bent on aggression and domination'.[1] *The New York Times* at about the same time quoted a senior official of the US administration as saying that 'Grenada, Beirut and the KAL airliner all served to confirm in the President's mind his own view of the world, that there was a common thread to all these events and it all led back to Moscow.'[2]

A majority of Americans appear to be preoccupied with a perception of Soviet expansion and communist influence, even to United States boundaries. (It is highly probable that these perceptions are mirrored in the perceptions of Soviet citizens who are aware of US military activities and political interventions on their boundaries.) This preoccupation may or may not be justified by Soviet philosophy and intentions. There is no ready means of knowing what these are: they are the unobservable data of foreign policy. The preoccupation may stem from what must now be regarded as a cultural prejudice against not only communism, but any form of socialism or planned egalitarianism that restricts individual achievement. The Soviet Union and communism are symbolic threats to important United States cultural values, whether or not these threats are real. The President, his advisers and the established élite that influence policy interpret world events within the theoretical framework that this cultural orientation creates. Where there is a rebellious faction within a state that seeks land reform, or where there is a government that tries to nationalise major industries, this must be, within this framework, directly or indirectly due to the influence of communism, and probably of the Soviet Union.

It is probable that conditions of feudalism and repression would promote movements of change towards alternative systems even if the Soviet Union did not exist. It may, on the other hand, be that the Soviet Union directly or indirectly instigates these movements. The point to be made is that the approach attributed to the President in *The New York Times* report is an inductive one. Given the cultural prejudice, given the theoretical framework, all events will be perceived and interpreted in ways that confirm the prejudice or theory. Any event anywhere that appears to threaten the legitimacy of the American system will reveal empirical evidence of Soviet malign intentions. Never will empirical evidence be found that contradicts the theory, and always there will be some evidence that can be interpreted as supporting it. This is not to say that the theory is necessarily wrong; but nor can it be argued inductively that it is valid.

Policies based on such inductive reasoning are self-fulfilling. A response to perceived threat sets in motion behaviours that are seen to threaten. The *Times* quotation is revealing in this respect. Grenada was one of very many countries in the world that had been torn by political strife under pressure of economic circumstances. In such circumstances rival remedies and philosophies are bound to emerge and be in combat. External interventions are likely. Sometimes they are sought. In this case an overture was made to the United States administration, but it was rejected. The rejection stemmed from a prejudice against the radical government and leader in control at the time as a result of a military *coup*. This rejection was an important factor in subsequent domestic developments that finally led to the decision to invade. In Beirut American forces acted outside the role of peace-keeping as it would have been defined had the forces been under United Nations control. They acted in support of one rival faction against others. They thus invited the assault on the United States forces which the President saw as being instigated by Moscow. In the KAL case, if there had not been systematic US surveillance, past spy-planes and Soviet fear of such incursions, the responses to this Korean incursion, based on a different theory, would probably have led to different behaviour.

From the President's perspective, all malign threads lead back to Moscow. From the Soviet perspective, no doubt, these same threads were all woven in Washington. The Soviet decision-makers also work within a theoretical framework based on prejudice and interpret inductively. In their view, one can deduce, the USA is bent on aggression and world domination. There is nothing they can do or say, save the self-destruct of their political system, that can create a basis for meaningful and rational discussion.

Whether the problem is in essence an analytical one arising out of the employment of power tactics in the pursuit of idealised goals, or wholly a sinister motivational one relating to the pursuit of power for its own sake, has to be made explicit and not allowed to remain a mysterious theoretical condition about which to speculate. It is this that is at the heart of East-West relations. Are the intentions of the other side malign? In which case there is no future in negotiations and attempts to avoid war. Or are they benign fundamentally, and dangerous only because of defensive tactics that are misperceived? The uncertainty gives rise to scenario-building based on worst-case analysis—a disaster in the thermo-nuclear age. A major endeavour is to find means of uncovering the hidden data of motivations and intentions.

For anyone not involved in strategic decision-making, and not finally responsible for the security of the state, an analytical and benign approach is intuitively reasonable. It assumes that both sides believe that they have reason, ideology, morality, history and legal norms on their side. Both are missionaries and equally idealistically inspired. The analytical hypothesis assumes that there is good-will and common objectives, but that there has been failure to resolve problems of relationships because of inadequate analysis and false perception.

If this were to be the case it would not be surprising in view of our generally inadequate knowledge base. The analytical hypothesis deserves consideration if only because we experience the same problem within domestic political systems. We do not know in the West how to handle inflation and unemployment. Hence we argue bitterly, and frequently attribute sinister motivations to those who advocate opposing policies. More directly relevant as an example, both in East and West there has been a failure to solve many aspects of the 'we-they' problem, even in the narrow confines of industrial relations. Indeed, an essential ingredient in any resolution of East-West conflicts is a mutual recognition of the complexities of organisational and political phenomena, and the inadequacies of existing theories, including the many versions of Marxism-Leninism, relative to these complexities.

If we were to assume that the essential problem between East and West were an analytical one, then certain conclusions could be drawn. It would be in the interests of both great powers to ensure that conflicts in spheres of influence and in areas of competition were resolved analytically so that stability were the outcome, even though the chances were the type of system resulting would not conform with either the socialist or capitalist model at the outset. For these purposes it would be important that both great powers were directly involved in the consultative processes that bring about such a result, instead of the present attempt to exclude each other from such negotiations. It would be in the interests of both great powers to try to ensure the stability of the other, to assist in the processes of change that each must inevitably undergo with technological advances and altered economic and political demands. It would also be in the interests of both actively to promote valued linkages between them as a means of control of the behaviour of each other.

However, we cannot afford to ignore the possibility that one or the other party to the socialist-capitalist conflict will behave in a sinister fashion, either as a tactic in pursuing defined goals, or as a means to power for its own sake. An analytical approach would be irrelevant and disastrous for one party if the behaviour of the other were malign.

The question at issue can be stated in simplistic terms without losing its content: how can each side in a major dispute determine the motivations and the intentions of the other during negotiations of all kinds and in interpretations of actions and statements? In even shorter form, what is the process whereby these unobservable, attributable data can be discovered?

Clearly, the traditional means of content analysis of statements, interpretations of behaviour, conclusions from historical analysis, and opinions based on case studies and experience of diplomats are of little profit. We have used these processes over hundreds of years and have all too frequently and disastrously arrived at inaccurate conclusions. There are philosophical reasons why this should be so, reasons that have been explored under headings of induction and deduction. Psychologists have directed attention to perceptual problems, transference and rationalisation. None of this has helped us do more than describe the problem: it has not helped solve it. The inductive approach has defeated us.

Finding a means of unearthing the hidden data of motives and intentions is a precondition of successful arms control negotiations, credible inspection plans, détente, peaceful coexistence and ultimately cooperation in resolving ecological and other problems both sides face. There can be no confidence-building and cooperation between East and West until motivations and intentions are exposed in a continuing process.

The Tunkin theory is itself a starting point. Are there implied norms that sanction interventions that inevitably result in power confrontations, in addition to the declared norms that should make peaceful coexistence possible? On the applied side, G. Arbatov's *The Soviet Viewpoint* is a well-researched and serious analysis of western policies perceived from a Soviet viewpoint in addition to being a statement of Soviet policies. There are similar western expositions in theory and practice. Can we assess these? How do we arrive at a process that enables both sides to distinguish between tactics and goals, propaganda and analysis?

The discovery of unobservable data finally rests on logical and analytical processes. Deceptions, rationalisations, hidden meanings finally come to light within a rigorous analytical interaction. However, we do not have the decision-making processes that enable this to take place in the interaction of governments.

It could be argued deductively that the Soviet-United States conflict reflects objective problems: the nature of change, the basic requirements of political systems, to what extent structures reflect the human needs of peoples, how we determine the best form of government even if we were to agree that human needs provided a given on which to assess policies and structures.

It could be argued empirically that the Soviet-United States conflict reflects objective motivational problems, the assessment of motives and intentions, how to differentiate between analysis and propoganda, benign and malign intentions.

While an adequate theory makes possible useful deductive reasoning and helps in posing the questions that need to be asked, a theory alone will not satisfy decision-makers on the two sides of the East-West ideological conflict. They rest on empirical data. There have to be continuing processes that help in an empirical way to answer the benign-malign questions. There have to be means of testing the benign-malign issue during negotiations of all kinds, especially during arms control negotiations. Academic analysis and deductions from it are not an acceptable basis of strategic policies that must assure security in all circumstances.

In the contemporary world the malign hypothesis dominates. Whether it is justified or not, it has been self-promoting: suspicion generates suspicion and inhibits cooperative initiatives. The malign hypothesis effectively presents those entertaining it from solving the problems they seek to solve, for example, arms escalation. All negotiations reinforce belief in the validity of the hypothesis. A government politically committed to the malign hypothesis cannot be seen to be taking positive initiatives for fear of being seen by the opposing power and by domestic publics as weakening under pressure. In matters of national security it is the duty of governments to adopt, if not a worst-case analysis, a most cautious approach to any relationships that appear to be threatening.

This poses a dilemma. Probably there cannot be progress on arms control until there is a reduced felt need for arms. But there cannot be a reduced felt need for arms unless the benign analysis is adopted and positive steps are taken to endeavour to resolve problems of change that occur within and between nations.

We do not *know* for certain whether states are aggressive or are, on the other hand, acting in defence against a perceived threat. We do not *know* whether values attached to relationships help to control behaviour. We do not *know* whether threat to national values is in origin international or national. These are still realms of uncertainty on which we are at present forced to base policies. Decision-makers cannot afford to go along exclusively with one set of assumptions or another. The consequences of a mistaken set of assumptions are too great. They have to evolve a 'fail-safe' strategy so that maximum benefit can be taken from positive and cooperative approaches, while at the same time ensuring that if the underlying assumptions are false, fatal consequences will not follow.

This seems to suggest the need for a deliberate building-up of a second-track policy running parallel with the first or strategic track. The old idea of a peace college (now revived with the US Congress Peace Academy proposal) was an intuitive response to this need. At present alternative approaches are confined almost entirely to scholars.

Government gives little support to these on funding, visa policies, trading, and in other ways. Something far more far-reaching would be required by government if a significant second track were to be laid down.

The two approaches, the malign and the benign, come together with the notion of a third-party or facilitating process at all discussions and negotiations. This is a technique that is now well developed in industrial and small group relations. The purpose, as we shall see, is to ensure that interactions between parties to disputes are analytical and avoid power-bargaining and all the tactics that accompany power-bargaining. It is a process in which a third-party panel injects information about conflict generally rather than about the particular issues being discussed. It is a process through which the parties to disputes or negotiations can discover the unobservable data of motives and intentions, and in the light of these, more accurately cost the consequences of their negotiation positions. Whether the assumption be in the malign or the benign framework, the process is relevant.

This is a process that government and officials find it difficult to accept. In it they can no longer operate from a given brief: perceptions and re-perceptions and costing of positions require flexibility and constant alteration of negotiating positions, which is difficult for officials acting under instructions. In any event, there is a felt need to preserve the role of government, which excludes professional third parties assisting officials with negotiation.

Until the processes are better understood, until there can be interactive decision-making, government could make far greater use than it does of scholars on both sides of the East-West confrontation. They are in a position to explore, to be flexible, and thus to canvass options that otherwise would not be presented and could not be explored.

Currently, relations between the Soviet Union and the United States are characterised by a level of mistrust that is difficult to contain even within day-to-day transactions. Arms control and other negotiations are likely to raise, and not lower, tensions as each side perceives the negotiating positions of the other as confirming the existence of malign intentions.

There is the possibility that what appears to be malign is a reasonable defence response to a perceived situation and is not otherwise malign. There is the possibility that both sides have a common desire to promote a peaceful relationship. Furthermore, there is the possibility that both sides agree fundamentally about the changes that are desirable in third nations which, in many cases, are just beginning to move towards independent development and are being held back by internal political conditions. There is the possibility that both sides could agree on processes of change that did not appear to be threatening to either and which would promote international stability.

The benign scenario needs to be explored without losing sight of possible malign intentions. One way is to move from power-bargaining in negotiation to analysis, with the help of a facilitating third party. Another is to make greater use of informal exploratory discussion at the unofficial scholar level. Both strategies would be helpful in uncovering the hidden and unobservable data of motivations and intentions which is a precondition to confidence-building and successful negotiation and cooperation.

NOTES

1. *The New York Times*, 11 November 1983.
2. *The New York Times*, 7 November 1983.
3. This book reads as though it were carefully researched and based primarily on western sources. It provides an exposition of the Soviet point of view that could be a rewarding basis for a searching dilaogue. However, western reviews treated it as a propaganda work.

PART IV:

PRESCRIPTION

In Part I of this book the approach was set out: it anticipated a paradigm shift both in the theory of behaviour and in the philosophical or methodological approach that would be adopted. The shift was from the traditional emphasis on the preservation of structures to an emphasis on the pursuit of human needs as the goal of political endeavour. The methodological shift was from an emphasis on 'fact', as determined within an ideological thought system, to an emphasis on deductions from this theory of behaviour.

In Part II we examined some of the domestic origins of international conflict that can be deduced from this theoretical framework. It was then possible in Part III to focus on the consequences of domestic policies for international politics. We finally drew attention to two specific problem areas that are significant for East-West relations. There is the problem of change and how to deal with this in a world sharply divided by ideologies that favour and resist change of particular types. There is also the problem of decision-making that is so inductive in practice, giving rise to the need to find means by which the hidden data of motivations and intentions can be revealed.

Prescription must address these two concerns. In practice

the two are one. Provided there were processes whereby change could be brought about which was mutually acceptable to those concerned and the great powers, there would be confidence-building and opportunities to observe and to test the good faith of the other. Provided there are interactions that enabled each to discover motivations and intentions, the change problem could be overcome.

In order to deal with these two related problem areas, we first examine the decision-making process and try to discover why it is at the national and international levels that decision-making has been so adversary. Then we turn to problem-solving techniques that are an extension of interactive decision-making processes.

13. Problems of Change

Throughout history, politics has been pursued and thought about as though it were the prerogative of élites, however appointed or selected. It was for them to determine forms of government, policies and values. There have been those who have a right to expect conformity and others who had a social and even a moral obligation to conform. This has been so in the factory, in national society generally, and in world society. As a consequence, there has been a strong bias in favour of the preservation of structures, resistance to change, justifications for the maintenance of systems even by force, even when there have been present, as a result of the political institutions that have emerged, gross inequalities of income and opportunity.

Our language reflects this. Revolt and rebellion have negative connotations, as do terrorism, deviance and dissidence. Rebellion is acceptable once it has been successful. It legitimises itself. On the other hand, terms which imply oppression of the individual, such as socialisation and integration, have positive connotations, despite the damage they can do to the development of the individual and group. We do not have a language of change that is positive in its connotation. We have no theories of change and a sparse literature on the subject as compared with the literature on law, socialisation and defence against change. Those who uphold a system, no matter how corrupt and oppressive, can be recognised as the 'legal' authorities; and those who seek justice and freedom are termed dissident or rebellious.

Our institutions do not favour change. They are designed to maintain societies in their existing form. Parliaments and courts can promote change, but only within the framework which they are committed to preserve.

This emphasis on preservation is the result of the evolution of societies and the social and political need for stability. A problem is created, however, when the need for stability is interpreted as a need to prevent change. Social and political stability in some circumstances is achieved only by change. The difference between the two concepts can be illustrated by changes in the design of aircraft that are made to bring about improved stability. United States policies in many countries seem to be based on a confusion between these two different notions. Law and order, the legality of government and resistance to movements of change can, in many circumstances, be sources of instability. The resistance to change in Poland was a source of instability in the longer term, even though change was prevented in the shorter term.

There appears to be in all cultures a language and a consensus that favours the preservation of the *status quo*, almost regardless of its nature. There is fear of the unknown.

One consequence is that authorities, facing situations in which change is demanded, have no options but to resist it. Faced with an inner-city riot, the symptoms, and not the origins, of the problem are attacked. In the case of a revolt in another country great powers, in particular, choose between various types of repression of opposition to and support for regimes under threat. There are no institutions, national or international, to which they can turn to resolve the conflict between those seeking change and those resisting it. There are, therefore, increasing levels of national and international conflict as structures become less and less relevant to societies.

It is not as though the problem has not been recognised. In 1965 Robert H. Kennedy said that the responsibility of our time was 'to lead a revolution—a revolution which will be peaceful if we are wise enough, human if we care enough, but a revolution which will come whether we will it or not'. To lead it towards freedom and justice was a formidable task, he said, but not impossible for us in our hemisphere: 'America is, after all, the land of becoming—a continent which will be in ferment as long as it is America, a land which will never cease to change and grow. We are as we act. We are the children and the heirs of revolutions.' He later said, 'if we allow Communism to carry the banner of reform, then the ignored and the dispossessed, the insulted and injured will turn to it as the only way out of their misery.' He once told the Senate, 'if we allow ourselves to become allied with those to whom the cry of "Communism" is only an excuse for the perpetuation of privilege, if we assist, with military material and other aid, governments which use that aid to prevent reform for their people—then we will give the Communists a strength which they cannot attain themselves.'[1]

In an article in *The New York Times*, Anthony Lewis commented* Everywhere in Latin America the policy is anti-Communism at any price. Washington winks at official mass murder in Guatemala. It cozies up to torturers in Chile and killers in Argentina. It ignores the appeals of our friends in Mexico and elsewhere for political negotiation.

The result of such a policy will be as Senator Kennedy predicted: to make communism more attractive to the dispossessed of Latin America, and improve the prospects for a revolution that is not humane. And there is another result about which he would have cared just as much: the darkening of the vision that we have of ourselves as a nation.[2]

These observations demonstrate the way in which domestic problems are attributed with external influences. At the same time, they highlight the need for institutions of change, both domestic and international, that can deal with problems of change before change is brought about by costly violence. These are not the institutions that are traditional, such as courts and parliaments, which are institutions designed to preserve. These are institutions that can assist all concerned in the costing of resistances to change. They are institutions that enable parties to assess their longer-term interests in promoting change by continuous processes rather than leaving change to violence that so often brings change, but not of the kind that all seek.

The great powers have a common interest in political and economic change that would make smaller states more stable. They do not disagree on this. They are fighting each other over the type of change and the method of change. It is in their common interest to ensure that there are orderly processes of change brought about by means that ensure that the goals sought are achieved. This is rarely the case when change is brought about, or prevented, by violence.

In the case of El Salvador, the USA sought some changes in the policies of the regime which was feudal and repressive. It did not achieve this because the regime knew full well that its existence, in the USA's view, was vital to US security interests. This was the situation in Vietnam also. No pressure on the Saigon government could persuade it to change.

The great powers get themselves into situations in which they become hostages to the small countries they seek to assist. It is in their mutual interest to encourage change by refusing assistance until there is change. However, this presupposes the means of change, institutions through which change can be agreed between conflicting parties. The opposing parties in El Salvador had no conception of the way in which their conflict affected great power relations. The United States perceived the activities of those in rebellion against this repressive regime as communist-inspired. If the parties had come together to reveal the nature of the problem, then it would have been plain to see that this kind of conflict would take place even if Marx had never been born and socialism had never evolved. The leadership in Poland seemed not to be able to cost the consequences of depriving its people of political and workplace participation. If they had come together it would have been plain for all to see that this situation would have occurred even if there was no capitalist system in the world. The USA apparently was not able to cost the longer-term consequences of its intervention in Chile. It apparently is not able to cost the consequences of its intervention in the Philippines and elsewhere where it props up regimes. What is required in each instance is a realistic costing by all parties concerned of their action and policies, and an exploration of options that would bring satisfaction at reduced costs. This is possible only when the parties are themselves face to face and can explore the unobservable data of motivations and intentions. They need to be assisted by others who can draw certain conclusions deductively from theories and experience of behaviour.

The great powers do not seem to realise that they effectively prevent face-to-face discussion between parties to disputes when they in effect guarantee, by arms and other assistance, the security of even the most repressive and non-legitimised regime. There is no need to negotiate, to change attitudes, or to cost the consequences of a conflict if support is guaranteed. The great powers become hostages to the smaller states and conflict escalates. It is in the interests of the great powers not to be placed in this position. One way is not to export arms without prior endeavours to resolve the conflict that makes arms necessary. Such arms control is probably more important than the control of the arms of the great powers, over which they negotiate fruitlessly.

As was noted in Chapter 12, in the background is the fear that change, though seen to be necessary, will not be to the liking of the great powers. This is especially the case with the United States. Jean Kirkpatrick, subsequently appointed by President Reagan as Ambassador to the United Nations, criticised the Carter administration for policies that advanced the well-being and preserved the political independence of developing countries. This would seem to be a reasonable policy. She articulated her fears thus:

The conceivable contexts turn out to be mainly those in which non-communist autocracies are under pressure from revolutionary guerrillas. Since Moscow is the aggressive, expansionist power today, it is more often than not insurgents, encouraged and armed by the Soviet Union, who challenge the *status quo*. The American commitment to 'change' in the abstract ends up by aligning us tacitly with Soviet clients and irresponsible extremists like the Ayatollah Khomeini, or, in the end, Yassir Arafat.[3]

The logical extension of this argument justifies American actions to protect repressive authorities and non-legitimised ruling élites. This poses a great dilemma. The only way out of the dilemma is to find means by which there is peaceful change acceptable to the parties involved in the domestic conflict, and agreement between the great powers not to intervene while conflict-resolving processes are being pursued.

A clue to what these processes are can be found in decision-making processes: it is in this area of enquiry that the solution to the change problem logically should be sought.

NOTES

1. This was from a speech made by Robert Kennedy, when on a visit to Latin America, before a group of Peruvian students.
2. Anthony Lewis made these comments in relation to the Robert Kennedy's speech. See *The New York Times*, 9 June 1983.
3. From Kirkpatrick's collection of essays, p. 41.

14. Interactive Decision-Making

The traditional decision-making concept is a simple, reactive, input-output one: Pavlov's dog sees meat and saliva flows. In the political field, the inputs are power inputs, such as resources and roles available to decision-makers. The outputs are the distributions of available resources by decision-makers according to their value systems. Applied to social organisations it is clearly an élitist concept: the assumption is that there are in any organisation those whose job it is to supply resources and those whose job it is to allocate them according to their value systems.

This traditional model has had inserted into it some complexities to account for experience: more and more interest has been shown in the actual processes of decision-making and the way in which there is feedback from the environment.[1]

However, all of these deision-making models or concepts, from the simplest stimulus response to the most complicated cybernetic processes, had in common those features that are inherent in the classical tradition. They all depicted reactive decision-making processes, and they all assumed a major power element in the process. They conceived decision-making as a vertical process, commands coming down from the apex of the pyramid that comprises a small élite, to the mass at the base whose obligation it is to obey. In so far as any protest response is communicated upwards, it is dealt with within the power framework which this structure implies, at least to the extent that available power makes this possible.

Clearly, this concept cannot readily include processes in which the values and motivations of those affected by decisions can be taken into account before decisions are taken. The cybernetic or feedback element allowed of some adjustments after responses by those affected. Furthermore, the concept of reactive decision-making is one that developed within the context of societies that were geared to maintain structures and not concerned primarily or even significantly with human needs.

This power or reactive concept of decision-making logically and empirically leads to making puzzles out of complex problems. A puzzle has a known outcome, as has a simple mathematical 'problem', a maze or a mechanical puzzle. A problem, on the other hand, has many possible outcomes, some of which lead to new problems in relationships; no final and definitive answers are possible. The strong and understandable tendency in political decision-making is to make puzzles out of pressing political problems. There is a need for achievement, certainty, decisive leadership, firm agreements. Where there is an effective power capability, complex behavioural relationships and organisational problems can be simplified into puzzles.

We have already noted how authoritarian leaders seek simple solutions to complex problems and attract political support as a result. Dissident behaviour and deviance can be suppressed without finding out their causes or resolving the underlying causes. In political life minority problems are frequently 'dealt with' by such means. They are defined as rebellion, and the definition becomes an adequate explanation of the behaviour and justifies the response. In the longer term ethnicity, identity and other influences emerge, often leading to violence, and this justifies even more repression while the original definition holds.

It is when puzzles are made out of problems that a legitimacy crisis emerges. In the world society there are many authorities that are wholly reactive in their decision-making and rest on military forces for the basis of their legal status. In the international system, great powers react in this same manner and endeavour to force their own decision on others. This is the nature of power-bargaining. Each side arrives at a bargaining decision, from which it is difficult to retreat within a bargaining process without adequate prior exploration and interaction. When the great powers confront each other over a situation in a third country, where unrest and political chaos invite change, they act separately and as adversaries without any exploration of possible solutions that suit both them and the parties concerned. Allies tend to act and decide only after some consultation.

In short, reactive decision-making processes themselves limit options and determine in advance of decisions the range of options that are possible. For example, courts make judgments within the bounds of legal norms: they cannot arrive at decisions that could in their view be 'just' if the law provides otherwise. Nor are they always free to take account of the values and motivations of all the parties concerned. Mediation seeks compromise: the mediator sees some point in opposing claims and tries to find a half-way agreement within the framework established by the rival claims of the parties. Bargaining confines negotiation to a set of proposals and the outcome is likely to reflect the relative bargaining power of the contestants rather than their longer-term interests. Attempts to settle disputes on the basis of a draft agreement limits options to the assumptions and notions inherent in the draft.

What we seek in the international system are decision-making processes that do not prejudice or limit outcomes in advance of discovery of possible outcomes that would satisfy the parties, in advance of an adequate analysis and definition of the total situation. In short, what we seek are realistic definitions of situations from which policies can flow. Definition is the end-product of analysis, not the beginning. Definition is possible only after interaction by the parties.

Instead, therefore, of a reactive model of decision-making, such as that described above, let us now consider an interactive model. Essentially it is a stimulus-response model; but there is an interaction between the parties that make decisions or are affected by decisions in any particular situation before decisions are made.

Inserted into any such model must be those features of the reactive model that are important to decision-makers. There must be some degree of certainty that the outcome is acceptable, that there can be no final decisions until an option is discovered that is acceptable, that there will be no compromise on important values, that final decision-making remains in the hand of decision-makers.

Such an approach to the making of decisions implies a set of assumptions that are distinctively different from those that underlie classical authoritative relationships. They include the assumptions that conflicts of interest, while appearing to the parties to be win-lose, are usually not so, perhaps never so, once perceptions, value hierarchies and costing have been analysed and explored; that there are processes that transform what appear to be win-lose conflicts into positive-sum ones; that there is a distinctive difference between settlement and resolution; that non-adversary-type decision-making in institutions opens up options not available to traditional adversary-type courts, parliaments and industrial institutions of decision-making.

Looking at decision-making from this point of view, there are three sets of models. There are those that make puzzles out of problems, that is, those that are interactive yet are still within a power framework. Second, there are those that recognise the need to satisfy legitimate aspirations, but at the same time rest finally on power or compromise that reflects relative power. Third are those that are problem-solving in the sense that they rest on analysis and seek outcomes that are positive-sum, satisfying the values of all parties.

This third set leads us to a consideration of problem-solving as a process in its own right, and the institutional forms it may take. Problem-solving has several distinct characteristics. First, the solution is never a final product. It is in itself another set of relationships that contains its own set of problems. For example, the problem of growth can be solved deliberately to give rise to problems of leisure that have then to be solved. A cybernetic process might achieve growth; but a set of unanticipated problems such as inequalities and class conflict could be the outcome. Second, problem-solving frequently requires a new synthesis of knowledge, new techniques and a change in theoretical structure. When deviance cannot be contained by coercion, a quite different strategy, based on a quite different analysis, is called for. Third, the system of interaction is an open one, that is, the parties are subject not merely to interaction among themselves, but to interaction with a wider environment over which there can be no control. It is the open nature of behavioural systems that is part of the problem. Employer-employee relationships are inevitably affected by the wider social and economic environment in which they take place.

It is because of these complexities that there has been a tendency to attempt to solve social and political problems by the more direct and simple reactive processes, that is, by making adjustments as and when necessary as responses and reactions occur. These complexities are also the reason why there has been such a strong tendency to deal with social and political problems by direct means of coercion.

The traditional approach in the social sciences is for the observer or analyst to stand at a point outside the situation or events under study. The situation is perceived by the observer within the framework of his/her normative standards, interpretations of behaviour, knowledge of history, sociology, politics and other aspects of the total situation. However, it is common patterns of behaviour which are the subject of study, not the common patterns of actors' overt behaviour as perceived by different observers. The only reality that is relevant is that of the actors, not the reality of the observer. It is only those involved in a conflict who can judge which variables are relevant, which patterns of behaviour are applicable. The conflict that is to be resolved is the conflict as perceived by those involved. Their interpretations of behaviour and events are part of the reality. Clearly they are likely to alter their perceptions and interpretations with increased knowledge. If the processes of resolution include increased information by reason of increased communication between parties to disputes or injections of information by a third party, then the nature of the reality will alter.

We are led, therefore, to seek processes in which observations of patterns of behaviour are made from within the situation by the actors themselves. These same conditions are those in which knowledge about patterns of behaviour can be fed back by a professional third party to those involved in a conflict, allowing them to select what they perceive to be relevant, and giving them the opportunity to alter their selection as new information seems to require.

These conditions suggest themselves. The parties to a dispute need to be placed in a situation that enables them to check their perceptions of each other, and the social order they are confronting, to assess the costs of pursuit of their goals in terms of loss of other values, and to explore alternatives that are available once this re-perception and reassessment have taken place.

There are many questions left open. Why should it be assumed that win-win outcomes are even a possibility? What theoretical and empirical evidence is there to suggest that the traditional win-lose definition of conflict is invalid? We have been concerned with shifts in thought, paradigm shifts, relating both to behaviour and to thought processes. To assert that the traditional win-lose perspective is false and that a win-win perspective of conflict is more realistic, is more challenging than was the flat-round earth paradigm shift.

This and other aspects of problem solving are the subject of the next chapter.

NOTES

1. *The Nerves of Government* was a major contribution by Karl Deutsch in the early 1960s. The feedback mechanisms of an automatic pilot provided a useful analogy that helped to transform concepts of decision-making.

15. The Notion of Win-Win

The traditional and consensus notion that conflict involves objective differences of interest stems from a belief that conflict is over scarce resources or fundamentally conflicting belief systems. Within this notion any expectation of win-win outcomes are mere utopian dreams. Marxist thinking, that so much rests on objective differences of interests within social groups, is part of this consensus notion that would seem to suggest win-win outcomes are unrealistic.

Yet, this utopian view is the position to which we are being led by contemporary thinking. Conflict is not over objective differences of interest that involve scarcity, at least not the kind of conflicts that are of concern in the international system. It is over more fundamental values of security and identity that are not necessarily in short supply, even though the tactics involved in their pursuit may involve shortages, for example, territory and power. Traditional approaches to conflict settlement have focused on allocations of goods that are in short supply, for it is over these that conflicts are thought to be fought. Conflicts are defined in these terms by the parties. Little attention has been given to the underlying causes, some of which the parties themselves may not be fully aware of while they are confined to a bargaining process.

A second traditional and consensus notion is that conflict

can be settled by imposing legal norms and by enforcing these against deviants. If, however, conflict is due to drives for security, identity and other human needs, then it would follow that these procedures are unlikely to succeed but are likely to lead to further conflict and protest.

These two consensus notions taken together, if false, have far-reaching policy implications. If conflict between persons and social groups, and conflict between persons and the state, is not due to scarcity but to more fundamental human aspirations, and if the division of a 'cake' of given size, or allocation of scarce resources by normative processes, is irrelevant to the nature of conflict, then much of the law-and-order framework on which societies rely for social stability, and much of the deterrent measures that are applied to deviance, are doomed to failure. At the international level, if the competitive problem is not due to scarcity of resources, and if threat does not deter when there are important values at stake, then the strategic policies of deterrence on which world society appears to rely, are unlikely to contribute to peace, and more likely to promote conflict to the extent that they frustrate the pursuit of human goals. The question whether there are such human needs, and whether they will be pursued regardless of consequences to self and to society because they are ontological drives, is a critical one.

While it seems likely that they are not fully aware of the significance of the paradigm shifts in which they are taking part, in all disciplines scholars are increasingly resting on assumptions that imply the probable existence of needs and wants that are universal and ontological. Experience and thought-processes seem to be forcing scholars into this framework: the search for explanation drives them to this new paradigm.

MacGregor Burns looked for the 'Wellsprings of Political Leadership' and found them in 'the vast pools of energy known as wants, needs, aspirations and expectations' that leadership must help those being led to achieve.[1] Sir Leslie Scarman, seeking explanations of city riots and other contemporary symptoms of unrest asserted that 'there is a natural law springing from man's own humanity which must be incorporated into the positive law of the state.'[2] Barrington

Moore, when trying to define the notion of justice, was driven to observe that 'it is obvious that human beings do have something that can be called innate needs.'[3] Peretz argued that the future of comparative politics rested on the assumption that there are some wants that are constant across systems.[4] Box has argued that the explanation of deviant behaviour is to be found in the denial of certain human needs, which he endeavoured to specify.[5] Wilson and Barash have endeavoured to incorporate the notion of human needs into biology.[6] Gurr and others have put forward theories of rebellion and war that suggest some universal features of behaviour at all social levels.[7] Weiner points to learning as just one of many ontological drives that must be satisfied if the individual is not to be disruptive of social organisations.[8] Sites observes that too much reliance has been placed on the socialisation process in the light of contemporary knowledge and empirical experience of the underlying causes of deviant behaviour.[9] In all these very different fields on study, scholars are arriving at a meeting point: universal, ontological needs that must be satisfied in the sense that individuals will be disruptive if they are frustrated in their pursuit.

This contemporary emphasis on human needs as a controlling element in social organisation is the logical extension of the earlier thinking of scholars such as Maslow, Thomas, Fromm, Bay and many others who were moving towards a general theory of behaviour in which to explain some particular phenomenon of interest to them.[10] What is new is the shift in emphasis. Sites expresses this by asserting that the influence in society of human needs is 'many times stronger than the influence of social forces which play upon man'.[11] In his view, society never completely conquers the individual. If necessary, 'individuals step out of the "real" world into a world of their own in an attempt to find fulfilment of more basic needs or at least to escape their complete frustration'.[12] The individual uses the legal norms as tools; but if these are inadequate others are invented 'if needs cannot be met by being honest, the individual tries something else'.[13]

As yet, there appears to be no consensus on what these

needs are, nor any agreed terminology. Needs, values and interests are sometimes used interchangeably, though a distinction is emerging that differentiates ontological needs from cultural values and personal interests. Sites has endeavoured to be more specific, and isolates eight needs: 'a need for response, a need for security, a need for distributive justice, a need for meaning, a need to be seen as rational (and for rationality itself), and a need to control'.[14]

We are faced, therefore, with the proposition that conflict at all levels may not be over scarce resources, such as territory, but over social goods that are not in short supply and, in fact, increase with consumption. The more security one party experiences the more, and not the less, does another party experience. The tactics of security—for example, the possession of a strategic position or the resources for thermonuclear defence—raise problems of scarcity. In thinking about conflict we have tended to confuse tactics and goals. Similarly, territory may be the means by which to achieve identity. Chapter 9, which dealt with the zonal system by which multi-ethnic societies might resolve their problems, was based on this notion.

It is this paradigm shift that is the explanation of the win-win concept inherent in conflict problem-solving. Once parties are in a position to separate tactics from goals, and to redefine their relationships, shared values are discovered. These values are not only held in common, but they are also values that increase with consumption. This is not utopian: it is behavioural realism that is superseding the so-called 'political realism' that rested on the assumption that power was the controlling force in social organisation, and from which assumption has flowed deterrent policies, coercive socialisation, authoritarianism and the consequences we are now experiencing in national and international societies.

It is in this context that we examine alternatives to the traditional settlement processes that are applied to conflicts between persons, persons and states, and states and states. They are the applied aspect of this theoretical paradigm shift in behavioural theory that is now waiting only consensus recognition.

There is, however, one aspect of this alternative approach

·to the handling of conflict which is not as yet fully understood. A theory of behaviour that argues that certain needs *will* be pursued, regardless of any force that might be used by authorities, suggests to anyone accustomed to traditional notions of law and order a kind anarchy. On the one hand, control theory holds that the individual will use all possible means to achieve these human needs. But there is the other side of the coin. In order to achieve human needs, in order to have identity and recognition in a social group, it is obviously necessary to have good relationships with those whose recognition is sought. There is a value attached to relationships. It is this value, not the processes of socialisation, that explain what order there is in society. If there is an absence of valued relationships, as is the case when a child is alienated from his parents, teachers and friends, then there are no constraints on behaviour, except to the degree that there is a value attached to relationships with a deviant cultural group. The same reasoning applies at other social levels. A state cut off from valued relationships has no motivation to observe the norms of the international society. Interdependence is an important control, not just because of the material gains, but for these reasons of social need. This aspect was also implied in the idea of a zonal system. It was argued that vetos would not be exercised thoughtlessly because of the value attached to the integrity of the state of which the national groups were a part.

NOTES

1. In his *American Political Science Review* article, Burns looked for these wellsprings in 'habit, motive, trait, instinct, need, drive, emotion, feeling, wish, purpose, desire, expectation, aspiration, claim, demand', p. 267.
2. See Scarman, *University of London Bulletin*, no. 39. 1977.
3. See *Injustice: The Social Bases of Obedience and Revolt*, 1979.
4. See Peretz, 'Universal wants', 1978.
5. The study of deviance, written in 1971, is one that has obvious implications for behaviour at the inter-state level, even though Box's concern was at the level of the individual in society.

6. This biological approach is resisted by many who label it determinism. But if there are universal human needs their final description will be made possible through biology.

7. Gurr's title, *Why Men Rebel,* is a general title: all men at all times in all cultures. The universal implication of needs that cross cultures is clear.

8. Most writers in this area seem to draw their conception of needs from developmental theory; that is, needs that are associated with growth. Recognition, stimulus and control are associated with learning at a very young age.

9. Sites must be regarded as amongst the most thoughtful of contributors to control theory. While he has contributed a general text on sociology, his early work, *Control, the Basis of Social Order,* is a major contribution.

10. See Bibliography.

11. p. 9.

12. p. 10.

13. p. 13.

14. p. 43.

16. Problem-Solving Processes

Problem-solving, we have argued, reflects a significant shift in thinking. This being the case, there is a need to clarify terms and to introduce a correspondingly new vocabulary. It is convenient to make a distinction between *settlement* of conflict and *resolution* of conflict. A conflict is *settled* when the outcome involves a loss for one side and an equivalent gain for the other, or a compromise in which all or some parties are to some degree losers. This is the position when, for example, parties are obliged to share a scarce resource, so that none is wholly satisfied. Some coercion is probably necessary to enforce such a settlement. A conflict is *resolved*, on the other hand, when there is an outcome which fully meets the needs and interests of all parties: it is, therefore, self-sustaining. This is the position when, for example, parties agree to exploit and to share a resource in such a way as wholly to satisfy values and interests of all.

We are familiar with the process of settlement, the legal and bargaining processes by which the proportions of gains and losses are determined. They include *judicial settlements, arbitration, mediation, conciliation* and *direct bargaining.* They reflect the application of legal and social norms, or the consequence of relative power. We know how courts, arbitrators, mediators and conciliators work, and we know the various forms of mediation and what the role of the mediator is.

The notion of conflict resolution, however, is unfamiliar to us. Conceptually, we can comprehend outcomes in which both sides win, but they are not part of our ordinary experience. Indeed, we do not have an appropriate vocabulary. The process could well be termed *problem-solving*. Whereas we have a clear image of a court or a bargaining table, we have no such image of a problem-solving institution. For want of a better term, those who experiment with problem-solving refer to a *workshop*. These two terms, problem-solving and workshop, are far from satisfactory because they have other meanings in English. Yet they have their merits. Problem-solving is a useful term because, when a conflict is settled rather than resolved, a problem in relationships remains even after the settlement. It is only when an option is discovered that satisfies the interests and needs of all parties that the immediate problem is solved. Problem-solving implies exploration, not merely the processes of bargaining. The word workshop is useful, because it suggests that all the parties concerned have to get down to the analytical job of problem-solving. They have to work at it. It may be time-consuming. As in the case with all workshops, there are skills and techniques, and there are tried and tested procedures. There is also the guidance of an experienced third party familiar with these processes.

It is useful to confine the term *negotiation* to the final stages of settlement or resolution. Once there has been agreement in principle, there remain the tasks of determining details and drafting an agreement. This narrow and more precise meaning of the term distinguishes negotiation from power-bargaining and from problem-solving.

The bargaining process is often assisted by a *mediator*. This term implies, clearly, a third party whose role it is to act as a go-between and to suggest a compromise allocation of gains and losses. Problem-solving does not imply either of these features of the mediation process. However, it rests no less on a third party, but one with a quite different role. The term we reserve for the third party in the problem-solving process is the *facilitator*.

Parties to disputes define them according to their own criteria: they are about wages, territory or other issues. But the declared issues are not necessarily the real ones. A wages dispute may be triggered by hostility to management or lack of job security. An international dispute which is basically about security may be defined by the parties by reference to a territorial claim. In a bargaining, mediation or settlement mode, the declared issues are those on which compromise is sought. In a problem-solving mode it is the issues underlying the declared issues that have to be discovered and analysed. For this reason it is useful to distinguish between *tactics* and *goals*. The claim for territory may be a tactic in the pursuit of the goal of security.

A more difficult distinction to make is that between *values* or *interests* and *needs*. This distinction is important to the explanation of why win-win outcomes may be possible. Values and interests relate to those goals of individuals, parties and cultures that are specific. They form a hierarchy of priorities and are subject to change in content and in hierarchical order. Needs relate to universal goals. Security, for example, is sought by all persons, in all cultures and in all circumstances. There are other needs that seem to be no less universal, such as identity. They are not subject to change, like temporary or cultural values and interests, nor are they necessarily in scarce supply. Their allocations can therefore, lead to win-win outcomes.

There appears to be a tendency to label conflicts by reference to the total situation. The United Nations refers to 'the Middle East' situation, 'the Cyprus' dispute, and appoints mediators in relation to these total situations. As a consequence, there is a tendency to group together all the divergent parties into just two opposing factions—Israelis and Arabs, Greek Cypriots and Turkish Cypriots (and the supporters of each side). But in any dispute there are many parties and issues specific to each of the parties. Consequently, before a total situation can be analysed and defined it must be broken down into its component parts. The issues are those that the parties declare, not those determined by any third party. Hence, in any particular situation it is appropriate to refer to a set of disputes comprising many *parties* and *issues*.

The settlement process assumes that there are objective conflicts of interest to be mediated; the goal is to provide the greatest possible material and psychological satisfactions to the parties. Underlying the assumption that there are objective conflicts of interest is an assumption that conflict is finally over finite goods, such as material goods or authority roles, that are in short supply. The processes of settlement are based upon these assumptions. They are essentially processes by which a limited quantity of material goods are shared according to legal norms or relative power, or by which an indivisible resource is allocated.

The ideal process of settlement has been regarded as one which is based wholly on legal norms, conducted by courts. These have mostly been unsuccessful, especially in international and industrial disputes in which important interests are at stake. The refusal of parties to seek or be bound by court decisions has led to a series of less formal and 'weaker' processes such as arbitration and, weaker still, mediation and conciliation. But even these weaker forms carry with them some obligation to accept the findings of the third party and are, for this reason, often avoided by parties to major political disputes. This leaves only direct power confrontation with consequences often costly to all parties.

The main reason why these processes are unacceptable, or often fail, is that parties to major disputes are not willing to hand over their decision-making to a third party. National leaders or responsible trade union executives cannot allow any third party, whether a court or a mediator, to make decisions that affect those whom they claim to represent. To be effective, conflict management processes must include high levels of participation by the conflicting parties and must leave final decision-making to the parties right up to the point at which the final agreement is negotiated. Traditional settlement processes provide neither opportunities for effective participation, nor effective control of the outcomes. In national and international courts, parties are represented by legal advisers and decisions are made by judges. In mediation the parties frequently do not even meet and the mediator has the role of suggesting a compromise.

In any aspect of life when we are faced with failure, it is time to reconsider our assumptions. In the case of the settlement processes, the means of allocating scarce material resources followed logically from the assumption that conflict is due to objective differences of interest in their allocation. Different assumptions lead logically to different processes.

The resolution process is a logical extension of another set of assumptions which may be more closely related to political realities. It is true that parties to disputes, whether industrial, international or other, regard their conflicts as being of a win-lose kind, and so set out to win. It is also true that in describing their conflicts they refer to goods in short supply—for example, wages or territory—or to symbols and roles that cannot be shared—for example, sovereignty or leadership. Courts and mediators have, in such conditions, no option but to accept the way parties define their conflict and arbitrate or mediate on this basis.

In practice, the stated issues rarely reveal the main goals and concerns. Wages demands are sometimes prompted by a sense of injustice, by feelings of resentment caused by 'we-they' relations, and other such rarely articulated motivations. Evidence that this is the case is suggested by the relatively low incidence of industrial conflict among small firms where there are close face-to-face relationships. International conflicts may be stated in terms of territory, as in the Middle East, or a foreign interference, as was the case in Iran. Underlying these overt grievances are often issues relating to security, recognition and identity. Settlement processes do not reveal these hidden concerns. Judicial settlements take into account legal norms, but not these underlying influences on behaviour.

Conflict may not be over scarce material goods, but over commonly held or universal goals such as identity, recognition, a sense of control through effective participation, security and such basic needs which are an ontological part of the human development process.

These needs are *social goals* that, unlike material resources, are not in short supply. The more secure the identity of a minority ethnic group, the more likely it is to accord recognition to others, and to cooperate within wider social and political systems.

If this is the case then, clearly, it is in the interest of all parties to ensure that the opposing parties achieve these social needs. Israelis, Greek Cypriots, Protestant Irish, white South Africans can best achieve their basic security goals by ensuring that their opponents have their own identity, recognition and security. This is not idealism: it is practical political realism, and it applies equally in industry and other social relations.

No coercive approach can produce security or lead to conformity. If identity, recognition, security and participation are fundamental human needs, repression, threat and coercion will not eliminate them. The resolution process must be such that these underlying motivations are brought to the surface and revealed by the parties. It must differentiate tactics from goals. It must correct misperceptions created by the language used, which often has to say one thing to a local population and another to others. It must give the parties the opportunity to explore options and not just to bargain over stated positions. This implies an analytical approach—the reason why the process has been labelled a workshop.

This analytical and exploratory approach to disputes cannot be undertaken by the parties alone. Experience has shown that even conflicts which arise within organisations created to resolve problems cannot be resolved by their members alone! There is always a strong tendency for persons and parties to lapse into a non-analytical bargaining confrontation. A third party seems to be essential. But this third party does not act as a go-between or suggest compromises, nor does it appeal to parties to observe legal norms and moral principles. It is skilled and well informed on patterns and theories of behaviour, human motivations and goals, the political values attached to status, role and other relevant subjects. Furthermore, it is a third party experienced in the process of facilitating direct communications between parties in conflict.

These are demanding qualifications. For this reason the third party in a resolution process is not an individual experienced in diplomacy or a professional lawyer, but must be a *group* of professionally qualified and experienced facilitators. But even this is not sufficient. Such a group needs to be in touch with a community of political and social scientists of all kinds to ensure that they can make available to the parties all relevant information.

There are some personal qualifications required in addition to professional qualifications and knowledge. These are primarily of two kinds. First, it is preferable that those who comprise the facilitating party do *not* have a specialised knowledge of the area or of the parties involved in the dispute. The reason for this is that it is essential that once the facilitator has tentatively determined the parties within the dispute that are most immediately concerned, the parties themselves define the dispute or conflict and determine the issues, values and motivations that are relevant. A regional specialist is likely to have his own preconceived ideas about the dispute. Second, facilitators need to have the capacity to identify with all parties on a non-judgemental basis, regardless of the apparent 'morality' and values of the parties. They are required to be, and to be seen to be, equally supportive of all parties. It is usual for the parties first to address the third party 'panel' and present their case. It is only when they perceive that the facilitating panel approves of both them and the opposition that the opposing parties recognise and address each other. This is the direct consequence of a supportive and non-judgemental approach. Not all persons have these abilities and can refrain from proposing and suggesting, at the risk of prejudicing their relationships with the parties.

The first task of the third party is to make a tentative judgement on who the parties are and what issues are involved. Typically, no conflict is between just two parties. There are usually divisions within parties and there are, almost invariably, external interests. Even the most apparently simple conflict generally involves many parties, each with its own special issues.

The initial judgement must be tentative since, once the process is under way, it is often revealed that those who seem to be the parties most involved and on whose agreement resolutions rests, are not the most relevant ones. The guiding principle is that those parties whose transactions are most threatened or severed are those with whom to commence; subsequently broadening out step-by-step. To take the case of Cyprus as an example, the two Cypriot communities are the main parties, Greece and Turkey are on the boundaries of the dispute, and the UK, USSR and the USA, while indirectly concerned, are less involved. In the case of the Falkland Islands, the islanders and the Argentine government were the parties immediately and directly concerned; the British government had a legal interest that would have to be negotiated once the main parties had agreed. This would have more clearly been the case had the Falkland islanders been given independence. An agreement between the parties most involved is likely to be acceptable by other parties—not the other way around.

A second step is to invite representatives of the parties that seem to be most immediately affected to a discussion, while at the same time taking steps to ensure that all other parties claiming an interest appreciate that their views and interests will not be neglected in subsequent discussions.

A legitimised body which, like the Red Cross, has a reputation for professionalism and success, attracts invitations from parties to a dispute. Even so, encouragement by other states is necessary, especially in conditions in which parties to disputes are guaranteed support by external powers. There are compelling reasons both why great powers are likely to give this encouragement and why smaller states would then respond. Conflicts within the spheres of interest of the great powers can readily spill over into a great power dispute. It is in the interests of all states, great and small, to deal both with problems of change within states and relations between states by means which do not risk escalation of conflict between the thermonuclear powers. The tendency in diplomatic negotiation is to endeavour to keep other powers out of conflicts which occur within a specific sphere of interest. In a conflict resolution process the direct involvement of scholars and advisers from powerful states is functional, and part of the wider endeavour to limit conflict and to establish cooperation and confidence.

Once the parties are assembled, the facilitators set the

stage. Parties will have come from a bargaining, and often violent, conflictual situation. They need to know what is expected of them in the non-bargaining and analytical setting. The supportive, non-judgemental role of the third party must be made clear.

The procedure is to invite each party to state its position. This takes a characteristic form. Both parties are likely to appeal to law, history and morality, directing this appeal at the facilitators. The parties, typically, do not address or look at each other. Then each party is invited to ask the other questions, strictly for information purposes, and not to engage in debate. After this, the panel is in a position to ask questions which seek to uncover aspects of the conflict that have not been touched upon—possibly unconsciously, probably deliberately.

The analytical process continues over some days. Little by little, the parties begin to address each other and gradually each begins to use the same terminology as the other in redefining its situation. The motives and interests revealed often turn out to be identical for both sides—security, identity and so on.

During this process the panel needs to have frequent and adequate opportunities for private discussion. Different disciplines and different backgrounds lead panel members to identify different points. Different theoretical orientations suggest different programmes. They need to analyse the input from the parties, to synthesise it and to present it back to them. If the panel misinterpret it, the parties will make this clear and the process will continue. When the parties are satisfied with the redefinition, the groundwork has been completed for discussion of possible options.

There is a great danger that this initial process, which usually lasts a week or so, will alter the values and perceptions of the participants. This would make their 're-entry', their reporting back to those they represent, difficult and perhaps impossible. Paradoxically, it is often more functional if those opposing each other around the workshop table leave with as much antagonism, even though with greater understanding, as when they came. Agreement can then rest on a functional basis that, despite suspicion and cultural differences, satisfies the interests, needs and goals as perceived by the respective parties. They do not have to like or respect each other to agree.

One precaution the facilitators can take is to make clear when making arrangements with the parties that 'hardliners', even governmental oppositions, should be included in the teams. Re-entry sometimes depends on such political activists being able to claim a 'win'.

It is part of the role of the facilitators constantly to remind participants of their re-entry problem, of their need not to compromise on key values, and to maintain as close contact as possible with those they represent.

It would be a mistake to contrast too sharply the traditional settlement process and the resolution process. In practice, despite the conflicting assumptions, one merges into the other. For example, the American Arbitration Association, despite its name, has been moving strongly in the direction of facilitating resolution. Courts, in their handling of first-offenders and complicated social problems, now rely far more on advice from experienced social workers. Mediation itself more and more tries to promote interaction between parties, though this is difficult when the parties do not come face to face.

One way in which the transition can be promoted at the international level is to encourage practitioner-scholar cooperation. Indeed, the employment of the conflict resolution process at the international level frequently requires active cooperation between the two, for example, when parties to disputes believe that they are guaranteed external power support and have no need to undertake any transactions with opposing parties. In these circumstances, as is the case when governments or factions cannot afford, for political reasons, to be known to negotiate with the 'enemy', there are some special roles that can be enacted usefully by scholars or persons who cannot be identified with decision-makers. This is an aspect of what we term 'second-track diplomacy', to which we now turn.

17. Second-Track Diplomacy

Second-track diplomacy comprises two elements. It is 'diplomacy' by non-diplomats, or non-official persons who are in a position to represent the views of authorities and to interact with them. It is also a diplomacy that seeks to resolve problems on the assumption that the motivations and intentions of the opposing side are benign, the first or strategic and official adversarial track being pursued simultaneously on a malign assumption. This notion, perhaps first articulated by a practising diplomat,[1] is one that synthesises contemporary trends in thought that attach importance to the individual as the unit of explanation of political behaviour, and which stress the need for processes of conflict resolution that logically flow from these trends.

The transition that we are now experiencing from social policies based on allocations of values as determined by ideological élites, to social policies that are influenced by the ontological needs of persons and communities, is a dramatic and revolutionary one. It is this transition, and the inevitable defences that are made against it, that best explain the high levels of domestic violence and communal and inter-state conflict that are universal in contemporary world society. Turkish Cypriots demand their identity and recognition as an ethnic or cultural group as do Catholics in Northern Ireland, Palestinians, South African blacks, women in all societies, workers in Poland and employees in factories. It is in this framework that we need to analyse terrorism, race riots, mugging and threats of nuclear war. It is a transition that has been in process since human society commenced. It is evidenced in the long-term movements from slavery to more liberal forms of relationships. The difference between now and past periods is that a philosophical change has occurred and has been articulated. There is no longer acceptance of an inferior status as though it were a part of a natural order. No longer is it accepted that there are those who have some inherent right to expect obedience and others who have a moral obligation to obey. This transition period is bound to be one of intense conflict, domestic and international. Conflict will become more widespread and more violent. Yet we have not evolved means of handling conflict outside the coercive framework that was the product of the former philosophy. The great need now in political life is for such institutions. Their creation will be resisted; but failure to suppress and to coerce will force acceptance of conflict resolution processes.

It has always been widely accepted in western political thought and practice that violence, including warfare, is, in the last resort, a legitimate means either of bringing about change or of preserving an existing order. The view that war is a legitimate instrument of last resort stems from the belief that relations between nations are determined, finally, by the calculations nations make of their own interests, and the relative economic and military power at their disposal. A small power has limited means to pursue its interest; a great power has a dominating position. However, two great powers, each with an 'over-kill' capacity present an unprecedented relationship. In theory, there should be assured deterrence; in practice, the concept of deterrence has provided the dynamic force for continuing accumulation of destructive power on each side. There is, consequently, a crisis in thought and in policy. A seemingly universal and rational philosophy and the policies based on it, appear to be outmoded. Where do we go from here?

Let us commence with the proposition that despite the

logical consequences of the thermonuclear confrontation, no great power will be diverted from its deterrence strategies. Let us assume that disarmament is politically unrealistic: there will not be disarmament or even effective control measures at least until there is less felt need for arms.

If we accept this proposition then we need to consider steps towards establishing peaceful relationships as an accompanying or parallel approach to deterrent strategies. By this we do not mean a competing or opposing approach. On the contrary, this proposition implies that security and peace are not necessarily mutually exclusive as people imply when they attempt to make a frontal attack on arms strategies. Strategic policies and peace-making are both legitimate activities. They are compatible, mutually supportive and, probably, necessarily interdependent. The two approaches can be perceived as being in tandem or on parallel tracks, conveying governments towards the common goal of avoiding war.

This is a simple notion, but it needs to be elaborated because a tradition of confrontation has emerged between the two approaches. It is as difficult for 'doves' to appreciate that 'hawks' seek peace, as it is for 'hawks' to realise that 'doves' are being realistic in their predictions of catastrophe. Furthermore, because private people and organisations press for disarmament, governments perceive this to be opposition to their defence strategies and they resist the 'doves' to justify their own policies. The two tracks have usually been perceived as going in opposite directions, and an adversary relationship has been developed between them. This effectively prevents governments from pursuing the second track of positive steps towards improved relationships as an essential part of their first track or power strategies. This adversary relationship within states becomes magnified within alliances as less powerful members perceive themselves as being the pawns or battlegrounds to be used by the one thermonuclear power in its contest with the opposing one.

It is in the interests of governments to be seen to proceed along the second track while still pursuing an effective security policy. This second track, therefore, has to be not an attack on strategic policies, but part of those policies, part of the activities of government working with those not in government who may have some contribution to make.

A second track would seem to include a set of related activities that require a close working relationship between various governments and others. Four such activities would be relevant in addition to continuing official contacts:

(i) a continuing means of communication between the main protagonists at an unofficial level so that there can be exploratory discussion in private, without commitment, on all matters that give rise to tensions between major powers— internal conditions, problems occurring in developing states, energy programmes, arms limitations agreements and others.

(ii) a semi- or non-official organisation which can offer a problem-solving service for parties engaged in conflicts within and between nations.

(iii) a training centre for people undertaking such work.

(iv) a research establishment that provides the back-up for the techniques required in all these three areas.

There is at present no credible institution within the international system to which participants in a major internal dispute can turn should they wish to seek assistance in resolving the dispute. Such disputes are outside the jurisdiction of the United Nations. Yet internal disputes frequently have serious international consequences. Nor is there any effective means of handling disputes between states. In his 1982 Report, the Secretary General of the United Nations stated that, 'something must be done, and urgently, to strengthen our international institutions and to adopt new and imaginative approaches to the prevention and resolution of conflicts.[2]

There are two reasons why the United Nations has not lived up to the expectation that it would be more effective in dealing with international conflict. First, it quickly became a political organisation, and political organisations are not appropriate for conflict resolution. There are few disputes between states in respect of which members of the Security Council can agree to 'terms of settlement as it may consider appropriate'. Often the use of the veto prevents any action being taken. The second reason is that it has confined its endeavours to those processes that were contemplated when the Charter was drawn up, in 1945. At that time there was no understanding of 'resolution' as distinct from 'settlement'. Legal norms and power-bargaining prevailed, so that the emphasis was on judicial settlements, arbitration and mediation. But these methods often proved unacceptable to disputants because no state leadership could survive allowing a third party to determine its interests and values. Weaker forms of intervention, such as conciliation, have also been found to be inadequate. There has been a retreat to 'shuttle diplomacy', but this fails for the same reasons. Statesmen cannot compromise when compromise destroys what is perceived to be a national interest.

Since 1945 in industry and all group relationships there has been a general movement away from legal and quasi-legal processes, towards analysis of difficulties in relationships on a non-judgemental and problem-solving basis, with full and direct participation of all the parties concerned. Judicial processes and mediation have given place to processes that are essentially designed to facilitate communication between parties by providing insights into relationships. These include opportunities to clarify personal and group values and perceptions, and to acquire knowledge about motivations and relationships generally, on which basis a particular dispute may be redefined.

However, there has so far been no such development at the inter-communal and inter-state level. While judicial settlements of disputes and the more informal processes of mediation seem frequently not to be acceptable or not to be successful, the problem-solving approach has not been attempted, even by the United Nations. At present inter-national procedures adopted by the United Nations and by states acting alone fall between the two approaches. Mediation and shuttle diplomacy are neither legal processes nor do they promote the direct interaction of the parties concerned. They rest to a large degree on the 'ideas' of the mediator who seeks a compromise. They do not enable the parties to explore directly outcomes they would be prepared to accept.

The ordinary processes of diplomacy have also failed. Frequently, when international tensions are high, parties to a dispute are reluctant to contine consultations or even the exchange of diplomatic representatives. Typical of this behaviour is when parties break off diplomatic relations just when they are most needed.

The reason why diplomats are withdrawn and the traditional mediation processes fail is that disputants are not prepared to weaken their bargaining positions by 'recognising' the opposing party or by entering into discussions on any basis other than the one they establish. The Cypriot parties could not be brought together by official mediators because each would meet only on the basis of the rival constitution it supported. Britain would not meet with the Argentine until the latter's forces were withdrawn from the Falkland Islands. Israel will not meet with the PLO because this would give them status and recognition. This gives the mediator no option but to practise 'shuttle diplomacy'. Often he loses the confidence of all parties, particularly when he urges compromise and acceptance of *his* proposals.

The question arises as to whether there could conceivably be any institutional framework in which parties in conflict— even in violent conflict—can meet in the presence of a third party to analyse their relationship, and to explore options. The question can be posed in another way. Is there any institutional framework in which parties could meet without in any way prejudicing their bargaining positions, without attracting charges of appeasement, without committing themselves, and without making it appear that they are seeking peaceful solutions at the expense of important interests?

Any such institutional framework would have to be outside the realms of power political relations and, therefore, outside the realms of diplomacy and inter-state institutions such as the UN, otherwise problems of status and recognition would crop up.

Secondly, any such framework would have to be such that it enabled parties to explore without commitment, without implied obligations to arrive at solutions, probably without giving up any military or other bargaining position they might hold.

Thirdly, any such framework would have to ensure that the parties were and remained the sole decision-makers, with equality of free decision-making, regardless of their relative military and political power, right to the point of agreement.

Fourthly, any such framework would have to promote an outcome that not only satisfied the persons participating in the problem-solving process, but their own electorates, including their oppositions.

In the field of emergency and disaster there are the Red Cross and similar organisations whose services are sought by those affected by the catastrophe. Their legitimacy is not based on any inter-state agreement or state sponsorship. It is based on their professional status and the total control of their activities by the host state which has invited them. A conflict resolution or facilitating service would need to have its legitimacy similarly based on its professionalism and the service it could provide.

There is no such institution in world society today. There is no body to which parties to disputes can come—except informal religious and private bodies that frequently endeavour to mediate, usually in the traditional way. This is a serious gap. The question we are posing is whether the gap is bound to exist because disputants will always refuse to meet and to discuss their conflictual relationship, or whether the institutions and processes that are available are irrelevant and inappropriate. Is it possible to create an institution that meets the four exacting conditions referred to earlier? This is the entry problem, which is not solved until the parties themselves, on their own initiative, *seek* a service. It is probably a myth that parties in conflict prefer to fight it out. A more likely explanation is that they continue in conflict because they perceive no alternative. Until there is an appropriate institution, parties will not seek peaceful resolutions.

There have been occasions in which parties to disputes have met in an analytical framework. Because it is analysis and exploration that is required, these occasions have tended to be semi-academic, that is, meetings of scholars and practitioners.

For example, the Test Ban Treaty was explored at a 'Pugwash' meeting in Moscow in 1962 by a number of American, Soviet and other scholars who had direct links with their governments. In 1965 there was a meeting between nominees of the governments of Malaysia, Singapore and Indonesia during the violent Borneo dispute, at a time when official endeavours were failing. The 'third party' was a panel of scholars. Similarly, there was a meeting in 1966 between nominees of the Greek President and Turkish Vice-President of Cyprus at a time when the UN mediator could not persuade the parties to meet together. Since then there have been several meetings in this academic framework between parties to disputes, including Middle East parties, at a lower level of representation.

Such meetings presumably met the four conditions stated above: they did not raise political issues of status or recognition, they allowed the participants to explore options freely and without commitment, the procedures did not limit the free decision-making of the parties, and the options contemplated were recognised as being designed to satisfy, without compromise, the values and needs of those whom the participants represented. Since these quasi-academic meetings were possible, it would suggest that the belief that no resolution processes are possible is a false one. Can there be similar applications generally in world society?

NOTES

1. This is a notion articulated by J. Montville of the US Department of State. See Bibliography.
2. See 1982 Report, p. 5.

18. The Role of Scholars

The nature of conflict resolution requires academic inputs because it is analytical and exploratory. It requires injections of whatever knowledge and insights are available in the total area of behavioural studies. It is for this reason that a third party in a problem-solving workshop must be a panel of four or five scholars, each of whom is widely interdiscipinary. The complexities of conflict situations require a close association between scholar and practitioner. The situation we face in Soviet-USA relations is too serious for role rivalries. We cannot afford the prostitution of scholarship by scholars to cull favour with authorities, nor the defensive reaction of senior members of bureaucracies who cannot reasonably be expected to be in touch with recent thinking. European culture keeps governments and scholars at a distance. Practitioners are sceptical and resent the interventions of scholars. Scholars fear identification with the ideologies and policies of governments. This is less the case in many other societies. Indeed, Western Europe is beginning to be an exception. While some of these resistances are in evidence in the USA, closer links between government and scholars are developing. In the Soviet Union, China and the developing world, the interactions are closer. There are dangers and difficulties, and unless each side values the role and integrity of the other, a close association could be dysfunctional. Be this as it may, there will not be effective problem-solving in the area of high level conflict without such a partnership.

Scholars have some special attributes and role advantages that need to be exploited in this vital area of conflict resolution. First, they can interact readily without having to maintain policy positions and in circumstances in which, as scholars, they have a role and a personal reputation to maintain. In the 1962 inspection debate that took place in Moscow under the 'Pugwash' banner, between twenty or so Soviet and American physicists and others, all on both sides began by agreeing with the position that had been taken by their governments. In the course of days each one had to stand up and be counted as a scientist in the presence of other scientists in the same field. They finally agreed on issues over which they previously had been in sharp disagreement. In the human relations field the issues are far more complex. However, the same procedures are required so that there is a scientific scrutiny of even the most eminent scholars.

A second attribute is that scholars are accustomed to interacting on a non-disciplinary basis when working together on complex problems. There are few, if any, major problems, including unemployment and defence strategy, that can be resolved within the boundaries of any one or even a few disciplines. The probability is that the knowledge base is there, and that what is required is the means by which it can be brought together outside ideological commitment. The process itself extends the knowledge base.

There is in East-West relations a continuing exchange of ideas and information at non-official as well as at official levels, through meetings of scholars and diplomats. However, this is not supplementing diplomatic and official exchanges to the extent that is possible. Diplomatic exchanges are largely negotiating and even adversary. Diplomats represent policy positions and are required to pursue them. They are based on a win-lose assumption and do not often explore win-win outcomes of disputes and differences of interest. The typical professional association meets each year for a week or less. In the political area it is likely that there will be scholars from both sides of the ideological divide. In the discussions they have during the few hours allocated for any one topic, rarely can they get further than stating their opposing positions. The time necessary for exploration in depth is not available. Relationships of respect develop, which is a bonus, but options do not usually emerge that could be fed back into the decision-making process.

An institution that is needed is one that would make possible greater use of specialists, even a continuing seminar of scholars which would monitor world events and the writings and opinions of other scholars concerning these events. It would seek to provide a continuing review of developments in world society, especially relations between the USA and the USSR, and the thinking of scholars in relation to these developments, for the use of those engaged in policy formation and administration.

There are several reasons why this seminar form of communication across boundaries may prove useful and important:

(i) It is only in such a seminar framework that there can be a perception and analysis of the total relationships. Governments are broken down into departments, and issues are dealt with separately by specialists in particular areas. Yet the problems facing world society are complex and require a holistic view if resolutions are to be found. Ecological, economic and psychological dimensions enter into decisions in respect to particular issues and areas of concern. An astronaut's perception of world problems is required.

(ii) Even in respect of the particular, administrations do not always have adequate technical knowledge and must rely upon specialists to explore possible options, as was the case when physicists investigated problems in connection with the Test Ban Treaty. Such a seminar would have the capability of calling into consultation any relevant scholars.

(iii) A seminar can provide insights not possible within adminstrations just because there is discussion within an analytical framework. Such a framework provides a basis for agreement, or at least an analytical framework in which discussion can take place without political bargaining, and understandings can be reached.

(iv) Scholars are expendable. They can attempt to arrive at

solutions. If they fail, there are no political consequences. If they succeed, there is a basis for negotiation at an official level. This is particularly the case in respect of matters that are sensitive and need to be explored before there can be discussion at an official level.

(v) Scholars are in a good position to bring together in an exploratory analysis the representatives of conflicting parties, even when each refuses to recognise the other. Because it is an academic framework, protocol and bargaining stances relating to recognition and preconditions do not arise. For these reasons a continuing seminar provides a useful alternative or complementary diplomacy and means of communication. It is a means of discovering positions and options which can be fed back into administrations for their consideration. This is a continuing process. *Ad hoc* meetings of a few days at a time do not meet the requirements.

(vi) In the longer term, one of the main benefits from a continuing seminar, and the publications that it could publish, is to bridge the gap between the time an insight appears in scientific literature and the time it takes to be known and applied. At the present, this gap is up to thirty or forty years—publication, discussion, inclusion in teaching curricula and the recruitment of students into the administrative process. Short papers that are relevant politically can bridge this gap.

There is resistance to such proposals by professional administrators who believe that they are specialists, the experts. This reflects the traditional view that there are those who have a right to govern, that government is an élite right. The fact is that, in the modern world, public administrations are not sufficiently equipped to cope with the problems with which they have to deal. Foreign offices comprise 'professional generalists' and only a small proportion have specialist training in fields other than the law. Law is mostly concerned with the preservation of systems, rather than with their change and adjustment to circumstances. The self-conscious attempts by some political and administrative leaders to consult academics is embarrassing to both. This does not apply to technicians. Governments consult with engineers when they wish to build a bridge. Indeed, they offer a contract. Building human relationships seems to be regarded as the preserve of the generalist, as do arms negotiations, mediation and the handling of complex conflict situations.

Only failure will change this and, indeed, it is beginning to bring about a closer relatinship between administrator and specialist. But it is too late at that point of time to prevent the consequences of failure. The Soviet system has an advantage over the free enterprise system. There the research and scholarly institutions are effectively part of government and available to be consulted. The West has failed to bring about a similar link for fear of losing academic freedom.

Academic freedom is fundamental to advising and Soviet scholars lack this. But western scholars are also beginning to give their academic freedom away in exchange for consultation: the need for research funds and for consultative status are destructive of academic freedom. These problems should not be insurmountable. It is the role and duty of professional associations to make advice available. Advice should be sought through them. It is for them to ensure the preservation of that academic freedom that is necessary to ensure that the advice is worth having.

PART V:

CONCLUSION

So far in this study we have adopted the procedure of many short chapters without sub-headings, each dealing with an aspect of the total problem of Soviet-US relations and world politics in the longer term. Now we bring these together under several sub-headings: the problem of greatness; the problem of ideology; the problem of decision-making; the problem of domestic insecurities; the problem of change; the problem of motivation and intention; and the problem of process.

The size, industrial strength and the spheres of interest that have to be protected are important considerations in the relations of the great powers. Both are engaged in the same power game and accuse each other of malign intentions, even though both behave in much the same way in playing out this game. The factor of greatness has to be taken as a given: it will not change. Yet it has to be noted as a significant influence.

Similarly, there is a problem of ideology. It is another factor that has to be treated as a given, yet recognised and taken into account.

One significant variable that is not unchangeable in the longer term is decision-making that is reactive within an ideological framework and, therefore, not adequately analytical. There are serious reinforcing consequences of reactive decision-making, and it is not yet part of conventional wisdom that inductive thinking can be misleading and self-fulfilling and, in this sense, self-defeating. It has to be treated as a given and taken into account when considering prescription. Part of this decision-making problem is the influence of élites and of authoritarian personalities who can be relied upon to come up with simple solutions that make even more complex the problems with which they are dealing.

Underlying these factors of greatness, ideology and decision-making is the problem of domestic insecurity. This relates to system faults and failures to promote human needs, leading to defensive and repressive policies that spill over into the international system. While the two systems are likely to evolve towards some common alternative, this requires time. Hence time must be built into prescription.

The problem of change is, therefore, one of the more important aspects of the total problem of Soviet-American relations. Change is a problem in itself, it is a complex process requiring innovation and adjustment. In political life adjustment is usually at the expense of some interest group and is resisted. It is a major problem in conditions in which two rival political systems struggle for survival.

Change is not possible to manage when there are serious doubts as to motivations and intentions between the parties concerned. This problem of hidden data is one of the most challenging, but one of the most important to resolve.

The problem of process becomes, therefore, the final focus of attention. How can change be facilitated in the countries of the world society, within the two great powers themselves so that they become less fearful of each other, and in the relationships of nations, North and South, East and West, Christian and Muslim, and rich and poor?

These seven sub-headings provide the basis of a synthesis. The synthesis is found finally in a consideration of process, to which a separate chapter is devoted. Given all the complexities, how can there be change, adjustments and cost-benefit decision-making so as to avoid war and to establish a basis of peaceful cooperation in the world society?

19. The Problem Areas

THE PROBLEM OF GREATNESS

It is far from certain that East-West tension and conflict is, as popularly thought, a function of ideological differences. It could be that the significant source of tension among the great powers may be their greatness and, in particular, their relative stages of growth towards greatness. All great powers are, or have been, expansionist—expansion is a necessary prerequisite of greatness. Industrial, trade, communications and diplomatic expansion are inevitable features of growth. Rome, the United Kingdom, the United States and the Soviet Union have all gone through stages of growth that altered their relative pecking-order in international relations. China will also. Changes in technologies, environmental conditions and political and economic structures lead to uneven rates of development giving opportunities to lesser powers to catch up in terms of industrial output and political influence. To begin with there is a struggle for unmeasureable parity so that there can be equal participation and an absence of domination. This struggle, for reasons that are both psychological and systematic, becomes one for superiority. In growth in industry and in social and political organisations, there is ample evidence that technological capabilities are exploited to the full, despite possible reactions and consequences.

At the international level, a sphere of influence acquired by a developing state needs to be protected by extensions beyond the boundaries of this sphere. If there is the capability it will be so protected. Then these extensions require protection, until there are 'foreign bases' scattered far from the national boundaries. This expansion process, like all expansion processes, has inbuilt limits. Each extension is more costly than the last; there is the factor of political resistance in the penetrated regions. Once a state goes beyond what are regarded by world opinion as 'legitimate' security needs, political resistances are generated. In due course, it seems, competition between resources needed for expansion—armed forces, subsidies and foreign expenditure—and resources needed for the satisfaction of consumer expectations, give rise to domestic resistance that can be suppressed only in the short term. Finally, contractions take place in the foreign field under such foreign and domestic pressures. The United Kingdom seems to have gone through this process. Are there some systematic processes relating to growth at work in international relations which have very little to do with types of political systems and policies?

Whether such processes operate or not, it is clear that states, advancing in greatness, use their influence to alter the international system and to adapt it to their interests, while relatively declining powers seek to retain existing structures, spheres of interest and linkages. As a consequence, there are, and always must be at any one time, 'revolutionary' and '*status quo*' powers. Are East and West, the Soviet Union and China, accusing each other of essentially the same behaviour—the behaviour of great powers, the behaviour to be expected of states becoming powerful at relatively different rates, the behaviour associated with different stages of influence?

As part of this power politics struggle to promote spheres of interest, great powers engage in local struggles: Vietnam, Laos, Kampuchea, Cuba, Angola, Ethiopia, Afghanistan, the Philippines, El Salvador, to mention only some. In the post-imperial world, in which there are many newly-independent states, there are necessarily many internal liberation movements and attempts to change from oppressive, sometimes corrupt, regimes to ones that are legitimised. Left to themselves, these liberation movements would bring about change gradually, with a minimum of local violence. While both powers could probably accept political change by indigenous processes, for strategic reasons each must oppose liberation movements that have the support of the other. The result is that both major powers support liberation movements in the sphere of the other, and both defend regimes in their own sphere that could not survive without external support. The levels of violence associated with change are high as a consequence. Each side in the power struggle perceives the behaviour of the other, not as the logical and inevitable consequence of their own systematic power struggle, but as an intended threat.

A straightforward competition for allegiance and spheres could be manageable. However, whether they support one type of regime or another, both sides have found that they lose control over their client states once they give support. The USA pressed the Saigon government to modify its policies and widen its support; but Saigon knew that it was strategically important to the USA and did not need to prejudice its authoritarian position. In Afghanisatan, where political stability was important to the Soviet Union in view of events taking place in Iran, the Soviet-sponsored regime was deaf to pleas for policies that would broaden its political base. Several governments currently are inflexible in their domestic and foreign policies knowing that one or other great power is finally committed to them. Thus, the major power rivalry has its consequences throughout world society, creating increasing instability and situations that cause serious tensions, crises and wars. The major powers cannot control the consequences of their power rivalries.

Underlying power confrontations are serious domestic problems. As observed above, imperial powers appear to crumble once they over-extend their spheres of interest, once costs escalate to the point at which the 'middle class' suffer and the internal infrastructures are weakened. Both the USA and the Soviet Union are currently feeling these effects. In addition, both political systems have their own sources of internal dissent and disintegration. However, in a bilateral power struggle the result is not a progressive withdrawal on the British model. These internal consequences are readily blamed on the other side and, faced with internal defeat, and therefore with nothing to lose, one side or the other is likely to try to solve its internal problems by promoting the perception of an external threat and by the consequential external interventions.

In sum, the world situation is currently one in which both major powers are locked in confrontation which is not under their control. There are processes operating that are dysfunctional to both that are inherent in the power policies which both pursue. Neither can give way in their escalating deterrence strategies and in their rivlalries.

THE PROBLEM OF IDEOLOGY

Let us now look at the conventional wisdom that holds that the great power conflict is basically an ideological one. The rhetoric of both sides reflects this conventional wisdom; but there is a great deal of confused thinking and argument associated with it. The Soviet system was a product of its past as well as the result of a revolution against it. Russia had been invaded many times, it was authoritarian in the extreme, it has a culture that places authority in a special category and gives freedom its own special connotation. It is a developing economy. The charges made against it by western leaders are charges that could have been made had the revolution not taken place. Furthermore, the charges do not take into account valid charges that can be made against western systems. The concept of 'freedom' cannot be confined to freedom of the press and of expression which, in any event, are not universal in western-supported countries. Freedom includes freedom to be educated so there can be expression, freedom to obtain a job and to be provided for in all circumstances, freedom to live free of violence. The accusations and counter-accusations are not ideologically based: what is practice in many western-supported countries is condemned in the Soviet Union. The welfare state within a capitalist system is perhaps as much feared and opposed as socialism and communism. We have to look deeper for the sources of East-West conflict.

THE PROBLEM OF DECISION—MAKING

The link between ideology and reactive decision-making is a direct one. Previously, reference was made to the way in which a series of events was perceived by President Reagan as deliberate provocation by Moscow: Grenada, Beirut and the KAL airliner. In each case the Soviet could give the opposite interpretation.

The consequences of selective perception are all the more dangerous and self-fulfilling when there are involved authoritarian personalities and advisers who are not trained in the interpretation of complex data and the handling of complex situations. Elite pressures also tend to support simple explanations and solutions when they correspond to interests, as is the case when the use of force seems to be the most obvious course and when there are strong interest groups concerned with arms production and the employment it maintains.

THE PROBLEM OF DOMESTIC INSECURITIES

A national security policy has two related aspects. The first, and the more important in the long term, is internal or domestic peace and security based on justice. This, in turn, rests on effective political participation by all, cooperation between government and industry and workers in industry, the encouragement and use of scholarship and cooperation with local communities of all kinds. No state is threatened when its nationals value their institutions. Internal strength is a nation's main source of security.

Equally, no state can be secure against external threats, despite its strategic policies and its power, if its nationals do not value its institutions. Race and inner-city riots, terrorism, street violence, obscene inequalities of income and opportunity, corruption in high places, are symptoms of the failure of a system. This is a source of national insecurity that no defence policies can offset. Social instabilities of this kind require more and more repression and lead to the destruction of the system the repression was designed to protect. Furthermore, historically, the consequences of internal failures have been international conflicts. Great powers, in particular, tend to view social and political change in their spheres of influence as a threat to their own institutions which are not wholly just in their consequences. They believe that they can best defend their own systems by ensuring that their system failures are perpetuated in the systems of others.

The second aspect of security policy is a defensive foreign policy. This becomes a vital necessity when there is failure at home. Many countries in the contemporary world society are members of alliances and have large military forces at their disposal only because they are faced with internal opposition, because they are not legitimised authorities that can stand on their own feet through popular support. Internal instability and international tensions and conflicts are not separate problems: the one leads to the other.

It is for these reasons that we have argued that there is probably no such phenomenon as international conflict that is not a spillover of domestic problems. When the Soviet Union reacts against demands for participation in a neighbouring socialist country and alleges western provocations, this is not because of any likely western aggressive action, but because of internal insecurities at this stage of development of the Soviet system. When the United States reacts against demands in neighbouring countries for fundamental changes in the feudal systems there, this is not because of any possible threat to the United States from these countries, but because of the need to defend the free enterprise system generally that is beginning to face system problems that are leading to conditions of *un*development. Countries, small and large, within the spheres of influence of the great powers are almost all experiencing the same kind of problems. None has a solution to its internal problems that would not destroy the structures and interests they are committed to preserve. If, as seems likely, there can be no international peace and stability until each unit within the world system has resolved its internal problems, then solutions to global problems are a long way off. This is the magnitude of the problem of Soviet-USA relations.

To some degree this definition of the problem of world peace has to be taken as yet another given: there is little that can be done in the short term to alter domestic structures and policies to the extent required to secure a peaceful international system. On the other hand, there are so many acute domestic situations that threaten the relations between the great powers that some relevant action to prevent confrontations must be taken for security or survival reasons. Either changes must take place within these countries, or the great powers must find ways of isolating themselves from the ideological conflicts that are taking place within them. Perhaps both strategies are required. Furthermore, there are changes that are required within the systems of the great powers as they experience technological innovation and demands for the satisfaction of human needs. It may be that their mutual security rests on cooperation in resolving their own special systemic problems, rather than trying to take advantage of them.

THE PROBLEM OF CHANGE

The factors of greatness and ideology are givens, whether they are important or not. Reactive decision-making and domestic insecurities are not givens or static elements, but the time factor probably makes them almost wholly irrelevant as part of a prescriptive approach. They are relevant only in the longer term. To some extent time can be bought by a recognition that it is required, and by an understanding of the processes of change that must be followed. A policy shift from defensive responses seeking to maintain the *status quo*, and from competitive responses seeking to win an advantage in a situation of change, to a focus on means of change that are deliberate, agreed and acceptable, may be possible if there are international, institutionalised means of change.

Change is not a subject that has attracted the attention of scholars, let alone politicians. Philosophy and culture universally are oriented towards preservation against change. Even adjustment to change that is inevitable—changes in the weather, changes in technology, changes in population size—is traditionally a 'muddling through' rather than a planned and deliberate process.

In 1962 *Peace Theory: Preconditions of disarmament'* was published, in which it was argued that

The study of peaceful international relations is not the study of a peaceful relationship destroyed by change and later re-established after adjustments have taken place, along the lines of the equilibrium analysis of economics. It is the study of a relationship in which change continuously takes place, but by means which do not necessarily destroy a condition of peace.[1]

In this work, a distinction was made between 'primary change', that is, change brought about by non-human influences, and 'secondary change', that is, change brought about as a result of adjustments to primary change or deliberately for some reason of policy. It was argued that the second world war was the product of shortsighted and self-defeating adjustments to changes in technology that had disturbed the economies of Great Britain and other major powers which endeavoured to cushion the effects of technological change by denying markets to Germany and to Japan in particular.[2] However, this particular work was an exception: the tradition has persisted to focus on means of preventing adjustment to change and preventing political change itself.

It is this dynamic aspect of the international system that is missing from the Tunkin analysis. The socialist-capitalist international assumes that all states, once socialist or capitalist, remain that way, that there is no political evolution with development, that the world society can be held static in this sense. It is true that the great powers would like this to be so in their present confrontation. But it is also true that the confrontation is in part due to the fact that the world society is not, and can never be, of this static nature. The solution is not to divide the world or to make Third World countries pawns to be fought over; but to provide means of peaceful change in the direction of agreed goals that reflect the aspirations and needs of the peoples concerned.

THE PROBLEM OF MOTIVATION AND INTENTION

Closely associated with the problem of change is the problem of motivation and intention. Is it true that the Soviet Union seeks to dominate world society, as suggested by western leaders, and that American capitalism seeks to detroy socialism wherever it exists, as suggested by some Soviet spokesmen? Or is the reality that both seek to preserve systems that require change, and both demonstrate a concern for change elsewhere for fear of its consequences for their systems? How can motivation and intention be ascertained? Is there a real desire for arms reductions, or does one side or the other or both seek escalation of arms for its own purposes? The hidden data of motivation and intention must be revealed by some means or other before there can be any meaningful negotiation of cooperation in any field. There is no empirical way of getting at this data, for empirical evidence is selected and interpreted within an inductive framework, as has already been argued. Lie-detector tests are now being applied even in western administrations; but it is hard to imagine them becoming an accepted tool of inter-national diplomacy!

NOTES

1. See Burton, *Peace Theory*.
2. *Ibid.*, Chapter 3.

20. The Problem of Process

We are finally led to consider the problem of process: what procedures can be followed that cope with the problems of greatness, ideology, decision-making, domestic insecurities, change, and motivation and intentions? What processes can we evolve that take into account the givens or political realities, and assist in dealing with those aspects of inter-state relationships that are subject to change and adjustment?

Attention has been focused on arms control and strategic balances as a means to peace through deterrence. The attention of publics, scholars and governments have been diverted from other aspects of relationships that are more fundamental. This reflects an assumption that the solution to the problems of world peace and security lies in arms control and disarmament. It is more likely that there will not be any progress in arms control until there is a less strongly felt need for arms.

If this is the case, then it is necessary to consider steps-towards establishing peaceful relationships as an accompanying or parallel approach to arms control. By this is not meant a competing or opposing approach. On the contrary, this proposition implies that security and peace are not necessarily opposites: they are both legitimate activities, compatible, mutually supportive and, probably, necessarily interdependent. The two approaches can be conceived as being in tandem or on parallel tracks conveying governments towards the common goal of war avoidance and cooperative relationships. This second track has to be, not an attack on strategic policies, but part of those policies, part of the activities of government working with those not in government who might have a contribution to make.

Having in mind the list of problem areas discussed in Chapter 19, there are many second-track activities that suggest themselves, some perhaps of peripheral significance, at least in the short term. For example, there is the role of diplomacy and the training of diplomats and advisers to overcome the inductive decision-making problem. There is the wider question to consider, whether traditional diplomatic immunities are in the interests of open diplomacy and understanding. There is the role of smaller states and the ways in which they can contribute to negotiations between the great powers. There is the problem of communications generally, and the ways in which scholars and their professional organisations can be used to explore options without commitment to governments. There is the necessary endeavour to determine motivation and intention within the context of any negotiations. There is no end of steps that could be taken to ease tensions if there were opportunities for second-track diplomacy, which is possible only when there is some institutionalised framework in which the two tracks can be followed simultaneously. Contemporary approaches based on deterrence and security through power cannot be justified empirically or in theory; they are no more than holding strategies—and dangerous at that. Security is finally derived from resolving the fundamental problems that are at the root of conflict. This being the case, we are forced back to the means, first of discovering what these roots are, and second, of finding agreed means of dealing with them. It may turn out that motivations and intentions are malign, that there are objective conflicts between the two competing systems is inevitable. Whether this is so or not needs to be discovered by relevant processes.

We are not in a position to make proposals and programmes that are likely to be agreed between the two

competing powers. It is as irrelevant to do this as it is for
mediators to make proposals for the settlement of particular
disputes. It is the process by which options can be discovered
and explored that has to be invented. It must be a process that
does not threaten to weaken bargaining positions, that is
compatible with track one, that includes all parties
concerned, small and large, that is analytical and subject to
scrutiny by those who do not share élite interests, and that is
legitimised by its professionalism rather than by power.

This statement of the problem points to a major gap in the
institutions of international society. The United Nations is
not a problem-solving organisation. Its politics and processes
are adversary. Nor are traditional forms of mediation
problem-solving in character. Furthermore, it is likely that
there cannot be the required type of problem-solving
institution within an inter-governmental framework. The
factors that we have taken into consideration—authoritarian
personalities, the influence of the élites, the nature of reactive
decision-making and the adversary nature of domestic and
international decision-making institutions—are alone
sufficient to suggest that the complex problems of
international peace and security cannot be resolved within
the framework of government.

The second-track notion has two aspects. First, it seeks to
reduce the felt need for arms, while still maintaining that
sense of security that arms might give. The second is that it
mobilises resources outside government, without in any
sense being opposed to government and its security policies.

On the small scale of conflict between two communities or
two states, experience has been that there can be redefinitions
of relationships and win-win options discovered once the
common needs of security, identity and control are satisfied.
The same processes are required in analysing the more
complex global problems that are being faced by the great
powers and their allies. Bilateral negotiations on arms control
or any other problem are bound to be within a bargaining and
power framework, with escalated conflict the likely result.
They need to be facilitated, as do any other important political
negotiations. Furthermore, they are of concern to and affect
all peoples and countries. Great power relations are global in

their consequences. Smaller states have a role to play as facilitators, or at least in constructing the international institution that would make facilitation possible. For too long smaller states have assumed that great power relations are best conducted by them. Even bilateral arms control negotiations affecting the peoples of Europe have been left to the great powers with the minimum of consultation with European governments. Wisdom is not the monopoly of the great powers.

The institution that seems to be required is one in which there can be an analytical monitoring of world events, bringing to bear the most recent thinking and a high level of objective analysis, with a wide participation of countries representing different cultures and political systems. This immediately suggests breaking down both the separation of small and large states, and the separation of official and professional roles. The United Nations, being an organisation that gives pride of place to the great powers and which is governmental in character, is not in a position to do this. However, one of its bodies, established by resolution of the General Assembly, does meet these requirements. That body is the United Nations University, which makes a report to the General Assembly on its activities each year. It is a body that has not developed a strong profile; but its role has never been seen in this perspective. It could readily fulfill the role of exploring alternative conceptual frameworks (such as the zonal system already described) in which particular situations can be discussed and negotiated at an official level.

In a real sense such an institution is the modern equivalent of the International Court. It is not the application of legal norms which we now seek, but the alternative conceptual frameworks that make possible the resolution of conflicts of interest.

Conflicts can, for practical purposes, be separated into two sets: those between states outside the great powers whose conflicts, domestic and international, are likely to involve the great powers, and those directly between the great powers. In respect of the former the following propositions seem to be relevant:

(i) Conflicts can be resolved (as distinct from settled) *only* by the parties concerned and without the external imposition of proposals by any other power.

(ii) For this to happen the services of facilitators will be required.

(iii) In any conflict there are many parties and issues involved, all of which must be taken into account before there can be an acceptable resolution and negotiation.

(iv) Solutions cannot be discovered and negotiated until each party fully appreciates the concerns and claims of all other parties directly and indirectly concerned, requiring more direct and more analytical communication than has traditionally been the case.

(v) Negotiated agreements imply some degree of compromise or accomodation; but any agreements finally negotiated must meet without compromise the security and ethnic needs of all the peoples concerned. There are some core issues on which there cannot be compromise. Power bargaining has to be excluded at all stages for this reason.

(vi) Such exploratory interactions do not involve issues of recognition or carry any implications other than those inherent in a mutual willingness to explore relationships. Informal and non-official interactions may sometimes be expedient.

(vii) Facilitators should form a panel as no one person has the knowledge or skills required to conduct such exploratory discussions.

(viii) External powers with an interest in a dispute may avoid becoming hostages to their clients by insisting that such processes be undertaken as a prior condition to any assistance.

(ix) Regional organisations are the appropriate location for conflict resolution facilities and the appropriate bodies to take initiatives in bringing parties to disputes together.

With respect to relations between the two great powers and their allies, whose relationships are global and not within the range of any regional organisation, the following propositions are relevant:

(i) There is a need for a standing seminar on international relations that can examine most recent thinking on relations between states, behaviour, motivations and human needs, the handling of conflict and other related topics.

(ii) This same body would also monitor current events and direct the attention of regional bodies to situations of conflict and if necessary take initiates itself.

(iii) It would also monitor relations between the great powers and endeavour to interpret events and statements within the theoretical framework that it evolves.

(iv) There is a need for such a body to make available facilitators to parties in conflict and, also, to the great powers in their direct negotiations on arms and other matters in which power bargaining is counter-productive.

(v) Such a body could be a source of conceptual alternatives, training of facilitators, and a means of communication when ordinary diplomatic communication seems not to be effective.

(vi) The appropriate location for such a body is the United Nations University thus establishing a link between the United Nations and its members and the international community of scholars.

Let us finally return to the original proposition, that there cannot be arms reductions until there is a lessened felt need for arms. This implies, once again, the two-track diplomacy of security through arms and security through measures designed to lessen reliance on arms. The starting-point in creating conditions of confidence must be, if this proposition is valid, in the region of the second track.

It follows that an initiating 'summit' needs to be not about arms control and such strategic measures, but about the establishment of such institutions as have been suggested, designed to monitor world events, offer alternative channels of communication, provide facilitating services, and also about the norms of intervention and arms supply to third countries. A second step would then be to improve bilateral relations designed to be of mutual assistance in giving both political systems time for change and adaptation to new technologies and to demands for the pursuit of human needs.

Postscript

As has been made clear in the Preface and subsequently in this study, we are not concerned with ideological positions or idealistic ones: political realities are our concern. Processes follow logically from the analysis of the relationships that are our concern. The political realities are that there are certain human needs that *will* be pursued over time. They can be frustrated in the short term, at the cost of societal violence and self-destruction. Given the further existence of civilizations, the pursuit of human needs will force societies in the general directions that characterise human eoltion. The rate is an exponential one for reasons of communications and technologies of protest. Whether it be South Africa, Poland, El Salvador or Sri Lanka, Northern Ireland or Afghanistan, Philippines or Romania— there are forces at work, sometimes dubbed ethnic, sometimes class, but finally human, that will determine final outcomes. The costs of change will reflect resistance to change and an absence of the institutionalised processes of change that enable parties to be informed fully in their costings.

The study of global conflict and the domestic sources of international tension is the study of human reationships in all their aspects. Our simple and seemingly straightforward theories and practices have failed us. It is time to reconsider, reconceptualise and question our consensus beliefs. As practitioners and scholars our task is to see to what extent, if any, we can cut shorter the painful processes of social evolution, even though we may not be able to redirect them sufficiently, so that we can get from here to wherever 'there' is, with the least possible destruction of human goals.

Hence the approach in this study. We identified a theory of behaviour based on human needs as a starting point, and a philosphical approach that enables us to think out these difficult problems. We then looked at system faults to which such a theoretical framework directed our attention. The international consequences of such faults were not difficult to perceive and to deduce. Prescription is determined by the analysis of the complaint, and it seemed apparent that a no-fault and problem-solving approach was appropriate, rather than a competitive-power means of settling differences. The problem areas are self-evident within the theoretical framework with which we commenced. That framework will be subject one day to empirical verification and testing. In the meantime we are confused with terminology and the absence of clear and agreed definitions of human needs. We could not see, and we have not even named, the particles of the atom before we assumed their presence. On that assumption knowledge and practice could be built. An adequate theory of behaviour is a prerequisite for policy-making. It is also a prerequisite for reliable prediction. What this study confidently predicts is global conflict unless human developmental needs are pursued, and unless we thereby gain time in which to work out solutions to human problems rather than merely suppress them.

If we must find fault, if there is to be criticism, it is of scholarship, especially higher education and our failure to build a consensus that takes into account our constantly changing knowledge and conceptualisations. The role of the scholar is not that of self-serving servant to the politician. It is the special and usually unpopular role of mentor.

Bibliography

Alger, C., See *Cities in Globilization of Human Communities*, 2nd YOKE Symposium Report Yokohama 1982.

Arbatov, G. and Oltmans, W., *The Soviet Viewpoint* (Dod, Mead & Co. 1981).

Ashraf, S. A., See S. S. Husain

Barash, D. P., *Sociology and Behaviour* (Elsevier 1977).

Bay, C., *The Structure of Freedom* (Stanford University Press 1958).

Blake, R. R., Shepard, H. A. and Mouton, J. S., *Managing Intergroup Conflict in Industry*. (Gulf Publishing Co. 1964).

Box, S., *Deviance, Reality and Society* (Holt, Rinehart & Winston 1971).

Brecht, A., *Political Theory* (Princeton University Press 1967).

MacGregor Burns, J., 'Wellsprings of political leadership', in *The American Political Science Review*, LXXI, March 1977.

Burton, J. W.,   *Peace Theory: Preconditions of
                                   disarmament* (Knopf 1962).
Burton, J. W.,   *International Relations: A general
                                   theory* (Cambridge University
                                   Press 1965).
Burton, J. W.,   *World Society* (Cambridge
                                   University Press 1972).
Burton, J. W.,   *Deviance, Terrorism and War*
                                   (Martin Robertson, Oxford/
                                   St Martins Press, NY 1979).
Burton J. W.,   *Dear Survivors* (Frances Pinter,
                                   London & Westview, Colorado
                                   1982).
Burton, J. W. et al.,   *Britain between East and West*
                                   (Gower Press 1984).
Cuellar, J. P. de,   *The Report of the Secretary General
                                   of the United Nations, 1982.*
David Davis Memorial   *Report of a Study Group on the
Institute   Peaceful Settlement of International
                                   Disputes.* (David Davies
                                   Memorial Institute, London
                                   1960)
Deutsch, K.   *The Nerves of Government* (Free
                                   Press 1963)
Duncan Report,   *The Review Committee on Overseas
                                   Representation, 1968-9,*
                                   Misc. no. 24 (1969).
Enloe, C.,   *Ethnic Conflict and Political
                                   Development* (Little, Brown 1973).
Fisher, A. G. B.,   *Clash of Progress & Security.*
Form, W. H.   See J. Hubber.
Fromm, E.,   *May Man Prevail?* (Douglas
                                   1961).
Goulet, D.,   *The Cruel Choice* (Athaneum
                                   1973).
Greenstein, F.,   *Personality and Politics* (Markham
                                   Publishing Co. 1969).
Gurr, T. R.,   *Why Men Rebel* (Princeton
                                   University Press 1970).

Himmelweil, S., 'The individual as basic unit of analysis', in Green, F. and Nove, P. (eds) *Economics: An anti-text* (Macmillan 1977).

Holsti, O., PhD thesis 'The belief system and national images. A study of John Foster Dulles, (1962). References in *Political Psychology* vol.3. nos 3,4. p. 1-33.

Huber, J. and Form, W. H., *Income and Ideology: An analysis of the American formula* (The Free Press 1973).

Husain, S. S. and Ashraf, S. A., *Crises in Muslim Education* (Hodder & Stoughton 1979).

Karnow, S., *Vietnam: A history* (Viking Press 1983).

Keynes, J. M., *The General Theory of Employment, Interest and Money* (Harcourt Brace 1936).

Kirkpatrick, J., *Dictatorships and Double Standards* (Simon & Schuster 1982).

Kuhn, T. S., *The Structure of Social Revolutions* (The Chicago Press 1962).

Levi, I., 'Induction in Pierce', in Mellor, D. H. (ed.), *Science, Belief and Behaviour* (Cambridge University Press 1980).

Lindsey, R., *The Falcon and the Snowman* (Pocket Books 1979).

Lloyd, D., *The Idea of Law* (Pelican 1964).

Maslow, A. H., *Motivation and Personality* (Harper Bros 1954).

Mitchell, C. R., *Peacemaking and the Consultant's Role* (Gower Press 1981).

Montville, J., See *Forien Policy*, no. 45, 1981-2.

Moore, B., *Injustice: The social bases of obediance and revolt* (White Planes (Pantheon Books) 1978).

Morgenthau, H. J.,   *Politics Among Nations: The struggle for power and peace* (Knopf 1948).

Peirce, C. S.,   See I. Levi.

Peretz, P.,   'Universal wants: A deductive framework for comparative political analysis', in Ashford, D. E. (ed.), *Comparing Public Policies: New concepts and methods* (Sage 1978).

Popper, K.,   'Normal science and its dangers', in Lakatos, I. and Musgrave, A. (eds.), *Criticism and the Growth of Knowledge* (Cambridge University Press 1974).

Robinson, J.,   *Economic Heresies: Some old-fashioned questions in economic theory* (Basic Books 1971).

Rostow, W. W.   *Politics and the Stages of Growth* (Cambridge University Press 1971).

Scarman, L.,   'Human rights', in *University of London Bulletin*, no. 39.

Schwarzenberger, G.,   *Power Politics: A study of world society* (Stevens, 3rd edn 1964).

Sibley, M. Q.,   *Nature and Civilization: Some Implications for Politics* (F. E. Peacock Publishers 1977).

Sites, P.,   *Control, the Basis of Social Order* (Dunellen Publishers 1973).

Tunkin, G. I.,   *Theory of International Law*, trans. and with introduction by William E. Butler (Allen & Unwin 1974).

Weiner, B.,   *Human Motivation* (Holt, Rinehart & Winston 1979).

Wilson, E. O.,   *Sociobiology: A new synthesis* (Harvard University Press 1973).

Wolfers, A.,   *Discord and Collaboration* (Johns Hopkins University Press 1962).

Wright, E. O.,   *Class Structure and Income Determinants* (Academic Press 1979).

Index